A Primer on
Corporate Governance

Praise for *A Primer on Corporate Governance*

"This book makes a splendid contribution to the teaching texts in the corporate governance field. I am most impressed with the pertinence of the materials. It is almost like meeting old friends."

—Robert A. G. Monks, author of *Corporate Governance*

"The manuscript is well organized and well written. I would be comfortable teaching from this book. I could see it finding a market in executive courses of various types and also in graduate, even undergraduate, courses in corporate governance."

—Kenneth A. Merchant, DeLoitte & Touche LLP Chair
of Accountancy, University of Southern California

"Timely and interesting best describe the book. With corporate and NGO Boards rethinking their responsibilities as well as their risks this gives board members a much needed handbook."

—John W. Bachmann, Senior Partner Edward Jones

"There's a lot to like about this book: it strikes me as intelligently thought out, incredibly well informed, surprisingly humorous, and generally very well fashioned for the executive market."

—Rafael Chodos, Attorney at Law, and
author of *The Law of Fiduciary Duties*

A Primer on Corporate Governance

Cornelis A. de Kluyver

Masatoshi Ito Professor of Management and former dean
Peter F. Drucker and Masatoshi Ito Graduate School of Management
Claremont Graduate University

First published in 2009 by
Business Expert Press, LLC
222 East 46th Street, New York, NY 10017
www.businessexpertpress.com

ISBN-13: 978-1-60649-004-4 (paperback)
ISBN-10: 1-60649-004-4 (paperback)

ISBN-13: 978-1-60649-005-1 (e-book)
ISBN-10: 1-60649-005-2 (e-book)

DOI 10.4128/9781606490051

A publication in the Business Expert Press Corporate Governance collection

Collection ISSN: 1948-0407 (print)
Collection ISSN: 1948-0415 (electronic)

Cover design by Artistic Group—Monroe, NY
Interior design by Scribe, Inc.

First edition: January 2009

10 9 8 7 6 5 4 3

Printed in the United States of America.

Abstract

This book is a primer on *corporate governance*—the system that defines the distribution of rights and responsibilities among different participants in the corporation, such as the board, managers, shareholders, and other stakeholders, and spells out the rules and procedures for making decisions on corporate affairs. Corporate governance also deals with how a company's objectives are set and the means of attaining those objectives and monitoring performance.

The importance of this subject can hardly be overstated. As recent corporate scandals have shown and the current financial crisis reminds us, the efficacy of corporate decision making and our regulatory systems directly affect our well-being. Sound corporate governance not only *pays by producing value* for all stakeholders of the firm but also, even more importantly, *it is the right thing to do*—for investors, other stakeholders, and society at large. In other words, sound corporate governance is also a moral imperative.

This book is designed to help you become a more effective participant in the corporate governance system—as an executive dealing with a board, as a director, or as a representative of a company's other numerous stakeholders. The book contains two major parts, an epilogue, and appendices.

The first part looks at corporate governance from a macro perspective. It describes the U.S. corporate governance system and its principal actors and briefly surveys the history of U.S. corporate governance, including the wave of governance scandals that occurred around the turn of the century. The second part focuses on the board itself and its principal challenges: CEO selection and succession planning, the board's responsibilities in the areas of oversight, compliance and risk management, the board's role in strategy development, the issue of CEO performance appraisal and executive compensation, a board's challenges in dealing with unexpected events and crises, and finally, a board's most difficult challenge—managing itself.

The epilogue briefly looks into the future and deals with subjects that are just beginning to appear on boardroom agendas. It assesses the emerging global convergence of governance systems, requirements, and practices; it looks at the prospects of further U.S. governance reform; and it discusses the changing relationship between business and society and its likely impact in the boardroom.

Keywords

Corporate governance, boards of directors, shareholders, stakeholders, capitalism, Sarbanes-Oxley, regulation, Security and Exchange Commission, New York Stock Exchange, NASDAQ stock exchange, auditors, security analysts, credit rating agencies, CEO succession planning, CEO evaluation, CEO compensation, strategy, management, oversight, audit committee, nominating committee, compensation committee, takeovers, risk management, shareholder activism, corporate social responsibility, global convergence, chairman of the board, lead director

Contents

Preface

Writing this book has been on my mind for almost 15 years. In the early nineties—as dean of the School of Business Administration at George Mason University—I had the pleasure of co-teaching an executive course on corporate governance with Nell Minow, a pioneer in the field. This experience convinced me of the importance of this subject to our welfare and cemented my interest in this topic.

Years later, as dean of the Peter F. Drucker Graduate School of Management at Claremont Graduate University, I had the pleasure of facilitating a thoughtful discussion between another pioneer in the field, Robert A. G. Monks, and the venerable Peter Drucker on the future of the corporation. Again, I was struck by how important the efficacy of our corporate governance system, laws, and practices is to the vibrancy of our brand of capitalism. I also became aware how little time was devoted to this important subject in most executive and MBA programs—hence the need for this book.

I have many others to thank. A number of colleagues at the Drucker School, including Vijay Sathe, Dick Ellsworth, Jim Wallace, and Rafael Chodos contributed substantially with their perspectives and constructive criticisms. Ken Merchant, Deloitte and Touche LLP chair of accountancy at the University of Southern California, wrote a thoughtful review on an earlier draft and made many useful suggestions for improvement. I also benefited greatly from conversations with executives, such as A. G. Lafley, chairman and CEO of Procter & Gamble, and John Bachmann, senior partner of Edward Jones. And I am grateful to Robert Klitgaard, president of Claremont Graduate University, and Ira Jackson, my able successor as dean of the Peter F. Drucker and Masatoshi Ito Graduate School of Management, for their support.

I am particularly indebted to the late Peter Drucker. His guidance and friendship meant a lot to me. Considered by many as the "father of modern management," Peter's unique perspectives on modern capitalism and on the role of the private sector, nonprofits, and the government have helped shape the thinking of CEOs, academics, analysts, and commentators alike. I hope this book contributes to this process.

Since much of what goes on in the boardroom is hidden to the outside world, there is no substitute for firsthand experience. Many of the observations in this book are inspired by my own experience as a director of a NASDAQ and a private corporation, as well as by my consulting work with large nonprofits. These experiences have particularly sensitized me to the realities of the "sociology" of the boardroom, the powerful set of forces that guides group behavior, especially when the players are competitive, away from their own power base, and under strong peer pressure.

As aspiring authors quickly learn and seasoned writers already know, writing a book is a mammoth undertaking. Fortunately, I had a lot of encouragement along the way from my family and friends, and I take this opportunity to thank them all for letting me spend the time writing this book and for their words of encouragement. I am grateful to all of them and hope the final result meets their high expectations. It goes without saying that I alone am responsible for any remaining errors or misstatements.

Cornelis A. "Kees" de Kluyver
November 2008

Introduction

What Is Corporate Governance?

The tug of war between individual freedom and institutional power is a continuing theme of history. Early on, the focus was on the church; more recently, it is was on the civil state. Today, the debate is about making corporate power compatible with the needs of a democratic society. The modern corporation has not only created untold wealth and given individuals the opportunity to express their genius and develop their talents but also has imposed costs on individuals and society. How to encourage the liberation of individual energy without inflicting unacceptable costs on individuals and society, therefore, has emerged as a key challenge.

Corporate governance lies at the heart of this challenge. It deals with the systems, rules, and processes by which corporate activity is directed. Narrow definitions focus on the relationships between corporate managers, a company's board of directors, and its shareholders. Broader descriptions encompass the relationship of the corporation to all of its stakeholders and society, and cover the sets of laws, regulations, listing rules, and voluntary private-sector practices that enable corporations to attract capital, perform efficiently, generate profit, and meet both legal obligations and general societal expectations. The wide variety of definitions and descriptions that have been advanced over the years also reflect their origin: lawyers tend to focus on the contractual and fiduciary aspects of the governance function; finance scholars and economists think about decision-making objectives, the potential for conflict of interest, and the alignment of incentives, while management consultants tend to adopt a more task-oriented or behavioral perspective.

Complicating matters, different definitions also reflect two fundamentally different views about a corporation's purpose and responsibilities. Often referred to as the "shareholder versus stakeholder" perspectives, they define a debate about whether managers should run a corporation primarily or solely in the interests of its legal owners— the shareholders (the shareholder perspective)—or whether they should actively concern themselves with the needs of other constituencies (the stakeholder perspective).

This question is answered differently in different parts of the world. In Continental Europe and Asia, for example, managers and boards are expected to concern themselves with the interests of employees and the other stakeholders, such as suppliers, creditors, tax authorities, and the communities in which they operate. Reflecting this perspective, the Centre of European Policy Studies (CEPS) defines corporate governance as "the whole system of rights, processes and controls established internally and externally over the management of a business entity with the objective of protecting the interests of all stakeholders."[1]

In contrast, the Anglo-American approach to corporate governance emphasizes the primacy of ownership and property rights and is primarily focused on creating "shareholder" value. In this view, employees, suppliers, and other creditors have rights in the form of contractual claims on the company, but as owners with property rights, shareholders come first:

> Corporate governance is the system by which companies are directed and controlled. Boards of directors are responsible for the governance of their companies. The shareholders' role in governance is to appoint the directors and the auditors and to satisfy themselves that an appropriate governance structure is in place.[2]

Perhaps the broadest, and most neutral, definition is provided by the Organization for Economic Cooperation and Development (OECD), an international organization that brings together the governments of countries committed to democracy and the market economy to support sustainable economic growth, boost employment, raise living standards, maintain financial stability, assist other countries' economic development, and contribute to growth in world trade:

> Corporate governance is the system by which business corporations are directed and controlled. The corporate governance structure specifies the distribution of rights and responsibilities among different participants in the corporation, such as, the board, managers, shareholders and other stakeholders, and spells out the

rules and procedures for making decisions on corporate affairs. By doing this, it also provides the structure through which the company objectives are set, and the means of attaining those objectives and monitoring performance.[3]

The Evolution of the Modern Corporation

Corporations have existed since the beginning of trade. From small beginnings they assumed their modern form in the 17th and 18th centuries with the emergence of large, European-based enterprises, such as the British East India Company. During this period of colonization, multinational companies were seen as agents of civilization and played a pivotal role in the economic development of Asia, South America, and Africa. By the end of the 19th century, advances in communications had linked world markets more closely, and multinational corporations were widely regarded as instruments of global relations through commercial ties. While international trading was interrupted by two world wars in the first half of the twentieth century, an even more closely bound world economy emerged in the aftermath of this period of conflict.

Over the last 20 years, the perception of corporations has changed. As they grew in power and visibility, they came to be viewed in more ambivalent terms by both governments and consumers. Almost everywhere in the world, there is a growing suspicion that they are not sufficiently attuned to the economic well-being of the communities and regions they operate in and that they seek to exploit their growing power in relation to national government agencies, international trade federations and organizations, and local, national, and international labor organizations.

The rising awareness of the changing balance between corporate power and society is one factor explaining the growing interest in the subject of corporate governance. Once largely ignored or viewed as a legal formality of interest mainly to top executives, boards, and lawyers, corporate governance for some time now has been a subject of growing concern to social reformers, shareholder activists, legislators and regulatory agencies, business leaders, and the popular press.

Shareholders, increasingly upset about outsized executive compensation deals and other governance issues, argue that too many boards are beholden to management and neglect shareholder interests. CEOs complain that having to play the "Wall Street expectations" game distracts them from the "real" strategic issues and erodes their companies' long-term competitiveness. Employees worry about the impact of management practices, such as off-shoring and outsourcing on pay, advancement opportunity, and job security. Meanwhile, outside stakeholders, focused on issues such as global warming and sustainability, are pressing for limits on corporate activity in areas like the harvesting of natural resources, energy use, and waste disposal. Increasingly, they are joined by civic leaders concerned by the continuing erosion of key societal values or threats to the health of their communities.

Behind these concerns lie a number of fundamental questions. Who "owns" a corporation? What constitutes "good" governance? What are a company's responsibilities? To shareholders? To other stakeholders, such as employees, suppliers, creditors, and society at large? How did Wall Street acquire so much power? And, critically, what are the roles and responsibilities of boards of directors?

About This Book

This book sets out to answer these kinds of questions and to provide a framework for analyzing today's corporate governance challenges. It is written for executives who wish to prepare themselves to work with or serve on a board of directors and seek to broaden their perspective from a focus on management to one on governance. It is organized in two major parts, an epilogue, and appendices.

Part I looks at corporate governance from a macro perspective. In chapter 1, we describe the U.S. corporate governance system and its principal actors and briefly survey the history of corporate governance in the United States, including the wave of governance scandals that occurred around the turn of the century. Chapter 2 delves deeper into the philosophical questions of ownership and accountability and asks, "Who owns the corporation?" It contrasts the shareholder and stakeholder perspectives and tries to find common ground between the two. Chapter 3 focuses on the role of the board and provides an overview of recent trends in board composition, structure, and leadership. Chapter 4 takes a close look at the flurry of reforms adopted in the last 10 years. This analysis shows just how much effective corporate governance depends on a delicate balance of power—among shareholders, directors, managers, and regulators—and on properly aligned incentives, clearly defined accountability and transparency, and last but not least, a steady ethical compass.

Part II takes a micro perspective and contains six chapters—each focused on major board responsibilities: Chapter 5 discusses CEO selection and succession planning; chapter 6 takes up a board's responsibilities in the areas of oversight, compliance, and risk management; chapter 7 focuses on the board's role in strategy development for the organization; chapter 8 deals with the issue of CEO performance appraisal and executive compensation; chapter 9 describes the board's challenges in dealing with unexpected events and crises; and chapter 10 analyzes a board's most difficult challenge—managing itself.

Part III consists of an epilogue and looks at the future and deals with subjects that are just beginning to appear on corporate agendas. It analyzes the emerging global convergence of governance systems, requirements, and practices; it looks at the prospects of further U.S. governance reform; and it discusses the changing relationship between business and society and its likely impact in the boardroom.

PART I

Corporate Governance

The System and Its Purpose

CHAPTER 1

Corporate Governance

The Link Between Corporations and Society

The U.S. Corporate Governance System

Today's U.S. corporate governance system is best understood as the set of fiduciary and managerial responsibilities that binds a company's management, shareholders, and the board within a larger, societal context defined by legal, regulatory, competitive, economic, democratic, ethical, and other societal forces.

Shareholders

Although shareholders own corporations, they usually do not run them. Shareholders elect directors, who appoint managers who, in turn, run corporations. Since managers and directors have a fiduciary obligation to act in the best interests of shareholders, this structure implies that shareholders face two separate so-called principal-agent problems—with management whose behavior will likely be concerned with its own welfare, and with the board, which may be beholden to particular interest groups, including management.[1] Many of the mechanisms that define today's corporate governance system are designed to mitigate these potential problems and align the behavior of all parties with the best interests of shareholders broadly construed.

The notion that the welfare of shareholders should be the primary goal of the corporation stems from shareholders' legal status as residual claimants. Other stakeholders in the corporation, such as creditors and employees, have specific claims on the cash flows of the corporation. In contrast, shareholders get their return on investment from the residual only after all other stakeholders have been paid. Theoretically, making shareholders residual claimants creates the strongest incentive to maximize the company's value and generates the greatest benefits for society at large.

Not all shareholders are alike and share the same goals. The interests of small (minority) investors, on the one hand, and large shareholders, including those holding a controlling block of shares and institutional investors, on the other, are often different. Small investors, holding only a small portion of the corporation's outstanding shares, have little power to influence the board of the corporation. Moreover, with only a small share of their personal portfolios invested in the corporation, these investors have little motivation to exercise control over the corporation. As a consequence, small investors are usually passive and interested only in favorable returns. They often do not even bother to vote; they simply sell their shares if they are not satisfied.

In contrast, large shareholders often have a sufficiently large stake in the corporation to justify the time and expense necessary to monitor management actively. They may hold a controlling block of shares or be institutional investors, such as mutual funds, pension plans, employee stock ownership plans, or—outside the United States—banks whose stake in the corporation may not qualify as majority ownership but is large enough to motivate active engagement with management.

It should be noted that the term "institutional investor" covers a wide variety of managed investment funds, including banks, trust funds, pension funds, mutual funds, and similar "delegated investors." All have different investment objectives, portfolio management disciplines, and investment horizons. As a consequence, institutional investors both represent another layer of agency problems and opportunity for oversight. To identify the potential for an additional layer of agency problems, ask why we should expect that a bank or pension fund will look out for minority shareholder interests any better than corporate management. On the one hand, institutional investors may have "purer" motives than management—principally a favorable investment return. On the other hand, they often make for passive, indifferent monitors, partly out of preference and partly because active monitoring may be prohibited by regulations or by their own internal investment rules. Indeed, a major tenet of the recent governance debate is focused on the question of whether it is useful and desirable to create ways for institutional investors to take a more active role in monitoring and disciplining corporate behavior. In theory, as large owners, institutional investors have a greater incentive to monitor corporations. Yet, the reality is that institutions failed to protect their own investors from managerial misconduct in firms like Enron, Tyco, Global Crossing, and WorldCom, even though they held large positions in these firms.

The latest development in the capital markets is the rise of private equity. Private equity funds differ from other types of investment funds mainly in the larger size of their holdings in individual investee companies, their longer investment horizons, and the relatively fewer number of companies in individual fund portfolios. Private equity managers typically have a greater degree of involvement in their investee companies compared to other investment professionals, such as mutual fund or hedge fund managers, and play a greater role in influencing the corporate governance practices of their investee companies. By virtue of their longer investment horizon, direct participation on the board, and continuous engagement with management, private equity managers play an important role in shaping governance practices. That role is even stronger in a buyout or majority stake acquisition, where a private equity manager exercises substantial control—not just influence as in minority stake investments—over a company's governance. Not surprisingly, scholars and regulators are keeping a close watch on the impact of private equity on corporate performance and governance.

State and Federal Law[2]

Until recently, the U.S. government relied on the states to be the primary legislators for corporations. Corporate law primarily deals with the relationship between the officers, board of directors, and shareholders, and therefore traditionally is considered part of private law. It rests on four key premises that define the modern corporation: (a) *indefinite life*, (b) *legal personhood*, (c) *limited liability*, and (d) *freely transferable shares*. A corporation is a legal entity consisting of a group of persons—its shareholders—created under the authority of the laws of a state. The entity's existence is considered separate and distinct from that of its members. Like a real person, a corporation can enter into contracts, sue and be sued, and must pay tax separately from its owners. As an entity in its own right, it is liable for its own debts and obligations. Providing it complies with applicable laws, the corporation's owners (shareholders) typically enjoy limited liability and are legally shielded from the corporation's liabilities and debts.

The existence of a corporation is not dependent upon whom the owners or investors are at any one time. Once formed, a corporation continues to exist as a separate entity, even when shareholders die or sell their shares. A corporation continues to exist until the shareholders decide to dissolve it or merge it with another business. Corporations are subject to the laws of the state of incorporation and to the laws of any other state in which the corporation conducts business. Corporations may therefore be subject to the laws of more than one state. All states have corporation statutes that set forth the ground rules as to how corporations are formed and maintained.

A key question that has helped shape today's patchwork of corporate laws asks, "What is or should be the role of law in regulating what is essentially a private relationship?" Legal scholars typically adopt either a "contract-based" or "public interest" approach to this question. Free-market advocates tend to see the corporation as a contract, a voluntary economic relationship between shareholders and management, and see little need for government regulation other than the necessity of providing a judicial forum for civil suits alleging breach of contract. Public interest advocates, on the other hand, concerned by the growing impact of large corporations on society, tend to have little faith in market solutions and argue that government must force firms to behave in a manner that advances the public interest. Proponents of this point of view focus on how corporate behavior affects multiple stakeholders, including customers, employees, creditors, the local community, and protectors of the environment.

The stock market crash of 1929 brought the federal government into the regulation of corporate governance for the first time. President

Franklin Roosevelt believed that public confidence in the equity market needed to be restored. Fearing that individual investors would shy away from stocks and, by doing so, reduce the pool of capital available to fuel economic growth in the private sector, Congress enacted the Securities Act in 1933 and the Securities Exchange Act in the following year, which established the Securities and Exchange Commission (SEC). This landmark legislation shifted the balance between the roles of federal and state law in governing corporate behavior in America and sparked the growth of federal regulation of corporations at the expense of the states and, for the first time, exposed corporate officers to federal criminal penalties. More recently, in 2002, as a result of the revelations of accounting and financial misconduct in the Enron and WorldCom scandals, Congress enacted the Accounting Reform and Investor Protection Act, better known as the Sarbanes-Oxley Act.

Most of the major state court decisions involving corporate governance are issued by the Delaware Chancery Court, due to the large number of major corporations incorporated in Delaware. In the 21st century, federal securities law, however, has supplanted state law as the most visible means of regulating corporations. The federalization of corporate governance law is perhaps best illustrated by the provision of the Sarbanes-Oxley law that bans corporate loans to directors and executive officers, a matter long dominated by state law.

The Securities and Exchange Commission[3]

The SEC—created to protect investors; maintain fair, orderly, and efficient markets; and facilitate capital formation—is charged with implementing and enforcing the legal framework that governs security transactions in the United States. This framework is based on a simple and straightforward concept: All investors, whether large institutions or private individuals, should have access to certain basic facts about an investment prior to buying it, and so long as they hold it. To achieve this, the SEC requires public companies to disclose meaningful financial and other information to the public. This promotes efficiency and transparency in the capital market, which, in turn, stimulates capital formation. To ensure efficiency and transparency, the SEC monitors the key participants in the securities trade, including securities exchanges, securities brokers and dealers, investment advisers, and mutual funds.

Crucial to the SEC's effectiveness in each of these areas is its enforcement authority. Each year the SEC brings hundreds of civil enforcement actions against individuals and companies for violation of the securities laws. Typical infractions include insider trading, accounting fraud, and providing false or misleading information about securities and the companies that issue them. Although it is the primary overseer and regulator of the U.S. securities markets, the SEC works closely with many other institutions, including Congress, other federal departments and agencies, self-regulatory organizations (e.g., the stock exchanges), state securities regulators, and various private sector organizations. Specific responsibilities of the SEC include (a) interpret federal securities laws; (b) issue new rules and amend existing rules; (c) oversee the inspection of securities firms, brokers, investment advisers, and ratings agencies; (d) oversee private regulatory organizations in the securities, accounting, and auditing fields; and (e) coordinate U.S. securities regulation with federal, state, and foreign authorities.

The Exchanges[4]

The NYSE Euronext and NASDAQ account for the trading of a major portion of equities in North America and the world. While similar in mission, they are different in the ways they operate and in the types of equities that are traded on them.

The NYSE Euronext and its predecessor, the NYSE, trace their origins to 1792. Their listing standards are among the highest of any market in the world. Meeting these requirements signifies that a company has achieved leadership in its industry in terms of business and investor interest and acceptance. The Corporate Governance Listing Standards set out in Section 303A of the NYSE Listed Company Manual were initially approved by the SEC on November 4, 2003, and amended in the following year. Today, NYSE Euronext's nearly 4,000 listed companies represent almost $30 trillion in total global market capitalization.

The NASDAQ, the other major U.S. stock exchange, is the largest U.S. electronic stock market. With approximately 3,200 companies, it lists more companies and, on average, trades more shares per day than any other U.S. market. It is home to companies that are leaders across all areas of business, including technology, retail, communications, financial services, transportation, media, and biotechnology. The NASDAQ is typically known as a high-tech market, attracting many of the firms dealing with the Internet or electronics. Accordingly, the stocks on this exchange are considered to be more volatile and growth-oriented.

While all trades on the NYSE occur in a physical place, on the trading floor of the NYSE, the NASDAQ is defined by a telecommunications network. The fundamental difference between the NYSE and NASDAQ, therefore, is in the way securities on the exchanges are transacted between buyers and sellers. The NASDAQ is a dealer's market in which market participants buy and sell from a dealer (the market maker). The NYSE is an auction market, in which individuals typically buy from and sell to one another based on an auction price.

Prior to March 8, 2006, a major difference between these two exchanges was their type of ownership: the NASDAQ exchange was listed as a publicly traded corporation, while the NYSE was private. In March of 2006, however, the NYSE went public after being a not-for-profit exchange for nearly 214 years. In the following year, NYSE Euronext—a holding company—was created as part of the merger of the NYSE Group Inc. and Euronext N.V. Now, NYSE Euronext operates the world's largest and most liquid exchange group and offers the most diverse array of financial products and services (see NYSE Web site at http://www.nyse.com). It brings together six cash equities exchanges in five countries and six derivatives exchanges and is a world leader for listings, trading in cash equities, equity and interest rate derivatives, bonds, and the distribution of market data. As publicly traded companies, the NASDAQ and the NYSE must follow the standard filing requirements set out by the SEC and maintain a body of rules to regulate their member organizations and their associated persons. Such rules are designed to prevent fraudulent and manipulative acts and practices, promote just and equitable principles of trade, and provide a means by which they can take appropriate disciplinary actions against their membership when rule violations occur.

The Gatekeepers: Auditors, Security Analysts, Bankers, and Credit Rating Agencies[5]

The integrity of our financial markets greatly depends on the role played by a number of "gatekeepers"—external auditors, analysts, and credit rating agencies—in detecting and exposing the kinds of questionable financial and accounting decisions that led to the collapse of Enron, WorldCom, and other "misreporting" or accounting frauds. A key question is whether we can (or should) rely on these gatekeepers to perform their roles diligently. It can be argued that we can and should because their business success depends on their credibility and reputation with the ultimate users of their information—investors and creditors—and if they provide fraudulent or reckless opinions, they are subject to private damage suits. The problem with this view is that the interests of gatekeepers are often more closely aligned with those of corporate managers than with investors and shareholders. Gatekeepers, after all, are typically hired and paid (and fired) by the very firms that they evaluate or rate, and not by creditors or investors. Auditors are hired and paid by the firms they audit; credit rating agencies are typically retained and paid by the firms they rate; lawyers are paid by the firms that retain them; and, as we learned in the aftermath of the 2001 governance scandals, until recently the compensation of security analysts (who work primarily for investment banks) was closely tied to the amount of related investments banking business that their employers (the investment banks) do with the firms that their analysts evaluate.[6] A contrasting view, therefore, holds that most gatekeepers are inherently conflicted and cannot be expected to act in the interests of investors and shareholders. Advocates of this perspective also argue that gatekeeper conflict of interest worsened during the 1990s because of the increased cross-selling of consulting services by auditors and credit rating agencies and by the cross-selling of investment banking services.[7] Both issues are addressed by recent regulatory reforms; new rules address the restoration of the "Chinese Wall" between investment banks and security analysts, and mandate the separation of audit and consulting services for accounting firms.

Corporate Governance Elsewhere in the World[8]

In Germany, labor unions traditionally have had seats on corporate boards. At Japanese firms, loyal managers often finish their careers with a stint in the boardroom. Founding families hold sway on Indian corporate boards. And in China, boards are populated by Communist Party officials.

The German and Japanese corporate governance systems are very different from that in the United States. Knowing how they function is important. The German and Japanese economies play host to many of the world's largest corporations. Moreover, their governance systems have had substantial spillover effects beyond their respective borders. Many countries in Europe, such as Austria, Belgium, Hungary, and, to a lesser extent, France and Switzerland, and much of northern Europe, evolved their governance systems along Germanic, rather than Anglo-American, lines. Moreover, the newly liberalizing economies of Eastern Europe appear to be patterning their governance systems along Germanic lines as well. The spillover effects of the Japanese governance system are increasingly evident in Asia where Japanese firms have been the largest direct foreign investors during the past decade. In contrast, variants of the Anglo-American system of governance are only found in a few countries, such as the United Kingdom, Canada, Australia, and New Zealand.

The German Corporate Governance System

The goals of German corporations are clearly defined in German corporation law. Originally enacted in 1937, and subsequently modified in 1965, German corporate law defines the role of the board to govern the corporation for the "good of the enterprise, its multiple stakeholders, and society at large." Until the 1965 revision, the German corporate law said nothing specific about shareholders. The law also provides that if a company endangers public welfare and does not take corrective action, it can be dissolved by an act of state. Despite the relatively recent recognition that shareholders represent an important constituency, corporate law in Germany makes it abundantly clear that shareholders are only one of many stakeholder groups on whose behalf managers must run the firm.

Large public German companies—those with more than 500 employees—are required to have a two-tier board structure: a supervisory board (*Aufsichtsrat*) that performs the strategic oversight role and a management board (*Vorstand*) that performs an operational and day-to-day management oversight role. There are no overlaps in membership between the two boards. The supervisory board appoints and oversees the management board. In companies with more than 2,000 employees, half of the supervisory board must consist of employees, the other half of shareholder representatives. The chairperson of the supervisory board is, however, typically a shareholder representative and has the tie-breaking vote. The management board consists almost entirely of the senior executives of the company. Thus, management board members have considerable firm- and industry-specific knowledge. The essence of this two-tiered board structure is the explicit representation of stakeholder interests other than of shareholders: No major strategic decisions can be made without the cooperation of employees and their representatives.

The ownership structure of German firms also differs quite substantially from that observed in Anglo-American firms. Intercorporate and bank shareholdings are common, and only a relatively small proportion of the equity is owned by private citizens. Ownership typically is more concentrated: Almost one quarter of the publicly held German firms has a single majority shareholder. Also, a substantial portion of equity is "bearer" rather than "registered" stock. Such equity is typically on deposit with the company's *hausbank*, which handles matters such as dividend payments and record keeping. German law allows banks to vote such equity on deposit by proxy, unless depositors explicitly instruct banks to do otherwise. Because of inertia on the part of many investors, banks, in reality, control a substantial portion of the equity in German companies. The ownership structure, the voting restrictions, and the control of the banks also imply that takeovers are less common in Germany compared to the United States as evidenced by the relatively small number of mergers and acquisitions. When corporate combinations do take place, they usually are friendly, arranged deals. Until the recent rise of private equity, hostile takeovers and leveraged buyouts were virtually nonexistent; even today antitakeover provisions, poison pills, and golden parachutes are rare.

The Japanese Corporate Governance System

The Japanese economy consists of multiple networks of firms with stable, reciprocal, minority equity interests in each other, known as *keiretsus*. Although the firms in a *keiretsu* are typically independent companies, they trade with each other and cooperate on matters, such as governance. *Keiretsus* can be vertical or horizontal. Vertical *keiretsus* are networks of firms along the supply chain; horizontal *keiretsus* are networks of businesses in similar product markets. Horizontal *keiretsus* typically include a large main bank that does business with all of the member firms and holds minority equity positions in each.

Like Anglo-American companies, Japanese firms have single-tier boards. However, in Japan a substantial majority of board members are company insiders, usually current or former senior executives. Thus, unlike the United States, outside directorships are still rare, although they are becoming more prevalent. The one exception to outside directorships is the main banks. Their representatives usually sit on the boards of the *keiretsu* firms with whom they do business. In contrast to the German governance system where employees and sometimes suppliers tend to have explicit board representation, the interests of stakeholders other than management or the banks are not directly represented on Japanese boards.

Share ownership in Japan is concentrated and stable. Although Japanese banks are not allowed to hold more than 5% of a single firm's stock, a small group of four or five banks typically controls about 20% to 25% of a firm's equity. As in Germany, the market for corporate control in Japan is relatively inactive compared to that in the United States. Bradley, Schipani, Sundaram, and Walsh (1999) found that disclosure quality, although considered superior to that of German companies, is poor in comparison to that of U.S. firms. Although there are rules against insider trading and monopolistic practices, the application of these laws is, at best, uneven and inconsistent.[9]

As Bradley et al. (1999) observe, although there are significant differences, there also is a surprising degree of similarity between the German and Japanese governance systems. Similarities include the relatively small reliance on external capital markets; the minor role of individual share ownership; significant institutional and intercorporate ownership, which is often concentrated; relatively stable and permanent capital providers;

boards comprising functional specialists and insiders with knowledge of the firm and the industry; the relatively important role of banks as financiers, advisers, managers, and monitors of top management; the increased role of leverage with emphasis on bank financing; informal as opposed to formal workouts in financial distress; the emphasis on salary and bonuses rather than equity-based executive compensation; the relatively poor disclosure from the standpoint of outside investors; and conservatism in accounting policies. Moreover, both the German and Japanese governance systems emphasize the protection of employee and creditor interests, at least as much as the interests of shareholders. The market for corporate control as a credible disciplining device is largely absent in both countries, as is the need for takeover defenses because the governance system itself, in reality, is a poison pill.[10]

As recent history has shown, however, the stakeholder orientation of German and Japanese corporate governance is not without costs. The central role played by both employees (Germany) and suppliers (Japan) in corporate governance can lead to inflexibility in sourcing strategies, labor markets, and corporate restructurings. It is often harder, therefore, for firms in Germany and Japan to move quickly to meet competitive challenges from the global product-market arena. The employees' role in governance also affects labor costs, while a suppliers' role in governance, as in the case of the vertical *keiretsu* in Japan, can lead to potential problems of implicit or explicit vertical restraints to competition, or what we would refer to as antitrust problems. Finally, the equity ownership structures in both systems make takeovers far more difficult, which arguably is an important source of managerial discipline in the Anglo-American system.

Corporate Governance in America: A Brief History[11]

Entrepreneurial, Managerial, and Fiduciary Capitalism

In the first part of the twentieth century, large U.S. corporations were controlled by a small number of wealthy entrepreneurs—Morgan, Rockefeller, Carnegie, Ford, and Du Pont, to name a few. These "captains of industry" not only owned the majority of the stock in companies, such as Standard Oil and U.S. Steel, but they also exercised their rights to run these companies. By the 1930s, however, the ownership of U.S.

corporations had become much more widespread. Capitalism in the United States had made a transition from *entrepreneurial capitalism*, the model in which ownership and control had been synonymous, to *managerial capitalism*, a model in which ownership and control were effectively separated—that is, in which effective control of the corporation was no longer exercised by the legal owners of equity (the shareholders) but by hired, professional managers. With the rise of institutional investing in the 1970s, primarily through private and public pension funds, the responsibility of ownership became once again concentrated in the hands of a relatively small number of institutional investors who act as fiduciaries on behalf of individuals. This large-scale institutionalization of equity brought further changes to the corporate governance landscape. Because of their size, institutional investors effectively own a major fraction of many large companies. And because this can restrict their liquidity, they de facto may have to rely on active monitoring (usually by other, smaller activist investors) than trading. This model of corporate governance, in which monitoring has become as or more important than trading, is sometimes referred to as *fiduciary capitalism*.

The 1980s: Takeovers and Restructuring

As the ownership of American companies changed, so did the board-management relationship. For the greater part of the 20th century, when managerial capitalism prevailed, executives had a relatively free rein in interpreting their responsibilities toward the various corporate stakeholders and, as long as the corporation made money and its operations were conducted within the confines of the law, they enjoyed great autonomy. Boards of directors, mostly selected and controlled by management, intervened only infrequently, if at all. Indeed, for the first half of the last century, corporate executives of many publicly held companies managed with little or no outside control.

In the 1970s and 1980s, however, serious problems began to surface, such as exorbitant executive payouts, disappointing corporate earnings, and ill-considered acquisitions that amounted to little more than empire building and depressed shareholder value. Led by a small number of wealthy, activist shareholders seeking to take advantage of the opportunity to capture underutilized assets, takeovers surged in popularity. Terms, such as leveraged buyout, dawn raids, poison pills, and junk bonds, became household words, and individual corporate raiders, including Carl Icahn, Irwin Jacobs, and T. Boone Pickens, became well known. The resulting takeover boom exposed underperforming companies and demonstrated the power of unlocking shareholder value.

The initial response of U.S. corporate managers was to fight takeovers with legal maneuvers and to attempt to enlist political and popular support against corporate raiders. These efforts met with some legislative, regulatory, and judicial success and made hostile takeovers far more costly. As a result, capital became scarce and junk-bond-financed, highly leveraged, hostile takeovers faded from the stage.[12] Of lasting importance from this era was the emergence of institutional investors who knew the value of ownership rights, had fiduciary responsibilities to use them, and were big enough to make a difference.[13] And with the implicit assent of institutional investors, boards substantially increased the use of stock option plans that allowed managers to share in the value created by restructuring their own companies. Shareholder value, therefore, became an ally rather than a threat.[14]

The Meltdown of 2001

The year 2001 will be remembered as the year of corporate scandals. The most dramatic of these occurred in the United States—in companies such as Enron, WorldCom, Tyco, and others—but Europe also had its share, with debacles at France's Vivendi, the Netherlands' Ahold, Italy's Parmalat, and ABB, a Swiss-Swedish multinational company. Even before these events fully unfolded, a rising number of complaints about executive pay, concerns about the displacement of private-sector jobs to other countries through off-shoring, and issues of corporate social responsibility had begun to fuel emotional and political reactions to corporate news in the United States and abroad.

Most of these scandals involved deliberately inflating financial results, either by overstating revenues or understating costs, or diverting company funds to the private pockets of managers. Two of the most prominent examples of fraudulent "earnings management" include Enron's creation of off–balance sheet partnerships to hide the company's deteriorating financial position and to enrich Enron executives and WorldCom's intentional misclassification of as much as $11 billion in expenses as capital investments—perhaps the largest accounting fraud in history.

The Enron scandal came to symbolize the excesses of corporations during the long economic boom of the 1990s.[15] Hailed by *Fortune* magazine as "America's Most Innovative Company" for 6 straight years from 1996 to 2001, Enron became one of the largest bankruptcies in U.S. history. Its collapse in December 2001 followed the disclosure that it had reported false profits, using accounting methods that failed to follow generally accepted procedures. Both internal and external controls failed to detect the financial losses disguised as profits for a number of years. At first, Enron's senior executives, whose activities brought the company to the brink of ruin, escaped with millions of dollars as they retired or sold their company stock before its price plummeted. Enron employees were not so lucky. Many lost their jobs and a hefty portion of retirement savings invested in Enron stock. Because the company was able to hide its losses for nearly 5 years, the Enron scandal shook the confidence of investors in American governance around the world. Outside agencies, such as accounting firms, credit rating businesses, and stock market analysts had failed to warn the public about Enron's business losses until they were obvious to all. Internal controls had not functioned, either. And Enron's board of directors, especially its audit committee, apparently did not understand the full extent of the financial activities undertaken by the firm and, consequently, had failed in providing adequate oversight. Some experts believed that the federal government also bore some responsibility. Politicians in both the legislative and executive branches received millions of dollars in campaign donations from Enron during the period when the federal government decided to deregulate the energy industry, removing virtually all government controls. Deregulation was the critical act that made Enron's rise as a $100 billion company possible.

In June 2002, shortly after the Enron debacle, WorldCom admitted that it had falsely reported $3.85 billion in expenses over 5 quarterly periods to make the company appear profitable when it had actually lost $1.2 billion during that period.[16] Experts said it was one of the biggest accounting frauds ever. In its aftermath, the company was forced to lay off about

17,000 workers, more than 20% of its workforce. Its stock price plummeted from a high of $64.50 in 1999 to 9 cents in late July 2002 when it filed for bankruptcy protection. In March 2004, in a formal filing with the SEC, the company detailed the full extent of its fraudulent accounting. The new statement showed the actual fraud amounted to $11 billion and was accomplished mainly by artificially reducing expenses to make earnings appear larger. After restructuring its debt and meeting other requirements imposed by a federal court, the company emerged from bankruptcy protection in April 2004 and formally changed its name to MCI Inc. Even as it emerged from bankruptcy, industry observers anticipated that MCI would need to merge with another telecommunications firm to compete against larger companies that offered a broader range of telecommunications services. The merger materialized less than a year later, in February 2005, when Verizon Communications Inc. announced its acquisition of MCI for about $6.7 billion in cash, stocks, and dividend payments. MCI ceased to exist as an independent company under the terms of the merger, which was completed in 2006.

As Edwards (2003) notes, these scandals raised fundamental questions about the motivations and incentives of executives and about the effectiveness of existing corporate governance practices, not only in the United States, but also in other parts of the world, including, What motivated executives to engage in fraud and earnings mismanagement? Why did boards either condone or fail to recognize and stop managerial misconduct and allow managers to deceive shareholders and investors? Why did external gatekeepers, for example, auditors, credit rating agencies, and securities analysts, fail to uncover the financial fraud and earnings manipulation, and alert investors to potential discrepancies and problems? Why were shareholders themselves not more vigilant in protecting their interests, especially large institutional investors? What does this say about the motivations and incentives of money managers?[17]

Because of the significance of these questions and their influence on the welfare of the U.S. economy, the government, regulatory authorities, stock exchanges, investors, ordinary citizens, and the press all started to scrutinize the behavior of corporate boards much more carefully than they had before. The result was a wave of structural and procedural reforms aimed at making boards more responsive, more proactive, and more accountable, and at restoring public confidence in our business institutions. The major stock exchanges adopted new standards to strengthen corporate governance requirements for listed companies; then Congress passed the Sarbanes-Oxley Act of 2002, which imposes significant new disclosure and corporate governance requirements for public companies, and also provides for substantially increased liability under the federal securities laws for public companies and their executives and directors; and the SEC adopted a number of significant reforms.

The Financial Crisis of 2008

Just as investor confidence had (somewhat) been restored and the avalanche of regulatory reform that followed the 2001 meltdown digested, a new, possibly even more damaging crisis, potentially global in scale and scope, emerged. While it has not (yet) been labeled as a "corporate governance" crisis, the "financial crisis of 2008" once again raises important questions about the efficacy of our economic and financial systems, board oversight, and executive behavior.

Specifically, as the economic news worsens—rising inflation and unemployment, falling house prices, record bank losses, a ballooning federal deficit culminating in a $10 trillion national debt, millions of Americans losing their homes, a growing number of failures of banks and other financial institutions—CEOs, investors, and creditors are walking away with billions of dollars, while American taxpayers are being asked to pick up the tab (Freddie Mac's chairman earned $14.5 million in 2007; Fannie Mae's CEO earned $14.2 million that same year). Not surprisingly, ordinary citizens who have seen the value of the 401K plans shrink by 40% or more are asking tough questions: How did we get into this mess? Why should we support Wall Street? Where was the government? What has happened to accountability?

While the causes of the current crisis will be debated for some time— Did we rely too much on free markets or not enough? Did special interests shape public policy? Did greed rule once again? Where were the boards of Bear Stearns, Lehman Brothers, and AIG? Were regulators asleep at the wheel? Incompetent?—one thing is for sure. Another wave of regulatory reform—this time possibly global in reach—is around the corner. And once again we will be asking the questions that prompted the writing of this book: What will be the impact on investor confidence? On corporate behavior? On boards of directors? On society?

CHAPTER 2

Governance and Accountability

Who Owns the Corporation? The Legal Debate

Do shareholders own the company? To most people, this idea is so axiomatic that the question hardly seems worth asking. However, the long-simmering debate about the age-old argument over the board's responsibilities to shareholders versus the rights of all company stakeholders flared up again recently, drawing attention once again to that central question.[1]

In the latest round of this debate, two leading corporate governance experts—Lucian Bebchuk, Harvard Law School professor and ardent shareholder-rights proponent, and Martin Lipton, founding partner of Wachtell, Lipton, Rosen & Katz and a stalwart defender of the view that it is management's prerogative to do what is in the best interest of the corporation—squared off in the pages of the *Virginia Law Review*.[2] The central issue in this debate is whether directors of a public company owe their primary fiduciary duty to its shareholders, as Bebchuk insists, or have to consider the prerogatives of all the stakeholders, as Lipton maintains.

Bebchuk (May 2007) cites a widely quoted 1988 ruling by the Delaware courts that "the shareholder franchise is the ideological underpinning upon which the legitimacy of directorial power rests" and points out that corporate law gives boards the authority to hire and fire management and set the company's overall direction. Next, he argues that since directors are expected to serve as the shareholders' guardians, shareholders must have the power to replace them. Thus, the fear of being replaced is supposed to make directors accountable and provide them with incentives to serve shareholder interests.

He continues by noting just how infrequently U.S. directors are actually challenged, much less removed, and concludes that shareholder power to replace directors in the United States is largely a myth. To make shareholder power real, he supports the proposal that directors be elected by a secret ballot open to rival candidates nominated by shareholders. What is more, to put them on an equal footing with the slate proposed by the board's nominating committee (usually with management input), he suggests that challengers should be reimbursed by the corporation if they receive a threshold number of votes.

Taking the opposing view and challenging the widely accepted argument that a company's primary goal is to maximize shareholder value, Lipton challenges the very notion that corporations are the private property of stockholders: "Shareholders do not 'own' corporations," he says. "They own securities—shares of stock—which entitle them to very limited electoral rights and the right to share in the financial returns produced by the corporation's business operations."[3] Directors, he argues, are not merely representatives of shareholders who have a legal responsibility to put investor interests first. Instead, the role of the board is simply and dutifully to seek what is best for the company itself, which means balancing the interests of shareholders as well as other stakeholders, such as management and employees, creditors, regulators, suppliers, and consumers. He concludes that Bebchuk's notion that a board's primary fiduciary obligation is to shareholders is a myth of corporate law.

Focus of U.S. Governance Law: Conduct or Accountability?

Governance in the United States has evolved as a medley of federal law—including not only corporation law but also tax and labor law, among others—state law, and a series of codes of various self-regulating authorities ranging from the NYSE to the accounting industry. As noted in chapter 1, state law has traditionally been the ultimate arbiter of governance issues. In contrast, in the United Kingdom, corporate reform can be affected simply through an Act of Parliament.

This unusual history of governance law in the United States has created openings for different interpretation of a variety of its provisions. For example, the law not only identifies shareholders as the "owners" of the corporation but also defines them as investors who receive ownership in the corporation in return for money or assets they invest. It stipulates that shareholders are responsible for "electing" a board of directors, the "operators" of the corporation who have overall responsibility for the business of the corporation, but it does not meaningfully address the implementation of this statute. It also specifies that the board of directors rather than its shareholders "directs" a company's business and affairs.

Additional guidance about a board's fiduciary role is contained in statutes governing the role and conduct of individual board members; specifically those defining a director's obligation in terms of such principles as the duty of care, duty of loyalty, and the "business judgment rule." The *Duty of Care* requires directors to be informed, prior to making a business decision, of all material information reasonably available to them in the exercise of their management of the affairs of a corporation. The *Duty of Loyalty* protects the corporation and its shareholders; it requires directors to act in good faith and in the best interests of the corporation and its shareholders. The prevalent legal standard is that the Duty of Loyalty requires that the director be "disinterested," such that he or she "neither appears on both sides of a transaction nor expects to derive any personal financial benefit from it" and his or her decision must be "based on the corporate merits of the subject before the board rather than extraneous considerations or influences."[4] The *Business Judgment Rule* protects directors from liability for action taken by them if they act on an informed basis in good faith and in a manner they reasonably believe to be in the best interests of the corporation's shareholders. The Business Judgment Rule does not apply in cases of fraud, bad faith, or self-dealing.

As long as these principles are adhered to and as long as directors are careful and loyal to corporate and shareholder interests, they have wide discretion to exercise their business judgment as they see fit. None of these principles provide clear guidance to the central question of who owns the corporation.

Corporate Purpose: A Societal Perspective

One reason that U.S. governance law is sometimes indeterminate is that the enormous differences between the two legal views described above reflect a broader, philosophical debate on the role and purpose of corporations in society. Indeed, opposing views on the purpose and accountability of the corporation—shareholders versus stakeholders, or private (property) versus public (social and political entity) conceptions of the corporation—have been part of the governance debate for well over 100 years.[5]

Shareholder capitalism, until recently prevalent mainly in the United States and the United Kingdom, holds that a company is the private property of its owners. From a legal perspective, the Anglo-American corporation is essentially a capital market institution, primarily accountable to shareholders, charged with creating wealth by exploiting market opportunities. *Stakeholder capitalism*, on the other hand, embodies a more organic view of the corporation in which companies have broader obligations that balance the interests of shareholders with those of other stakeholders, notably employees but also including suppliers, distributors, customers, and the community at large. Under this set of beliefs, the corporation is seen as an institution with a continuing purpose, and therefore, with a life of its own. Shareholders and wealth creation for owners do not dictate its priorities. Rather, a deep concern for employees, suppliers, and customers, and implicitly for its own continued existence, defines the corporate mission.

As noted in chapter 1, stakeholder capitalism can take different forms, reflecting the degree of commitment to different stakeholders. Germany's legal system, for example, makes it clear that firms do not have a sole duty to pursue the interests of shareholders. Under Germany's system of codetermination, employees and shareholders in large companies hold an equal number of seats on the companies' supervisory boards, and the interests of both parties must be taken into account in decision making. In Denmark, employees in firms with more than 35 workers elect one third of the firm's board members, with a minimum of 2. In Sweden, companies with more than 25 employees must have 2 labor representatives appointed to the board. These employee board members have all the rights and duties of other board members.

The situation differs somewhat in France. French firms with more than 50 workers have employee representatives at board meetings, but they do not have the right to vote. More conventional codetermination systems exist for former public-sector French firms that have been privatized; these systems can be introduced voluntarily by companies. In Finland, companies can also voluntarily adopt employee representatives on the board. Across the European Union (EU) as a whole, another type of worker participation in decision making is the works council, a group that has a say in such issues as layoffs and plant closures. A corporation with at least 1,000 employees, of which there are 150 or more in at least two EU countries, must have a "European Works Council."

The situation in Japanese firms also differs from that of the United States and the United Kingdom. Japanese executives do not have a fiduciary responsibility to stockholders, but they can be liable for gross negligence in performing their duties. At the same time, it is accepted practice in Japan that managers align their priorities with the interests of a variety of stakeholders. For example, a recent survey revealed that if Japanese executives feel that the company is going through a tough period financially, keeping their employees on the job is much more important than maintaining dividends to shareholders. Specifically, only 3% of Japanese managers said companies should maintain dividend payments to stockholders under such circumstances. This compares with 41% in Germany, 40% in France, and 89% in both the United States and the United Kingdom.

In the United States, these issues also continue to be debated. Some time ago *Reason* magazine featured a spirited debate among the late Milton Friedman, former senior research fellow at the Hoover Institution and Paul Snowden Russell Distinguished Service Professor of Economics at the University of Chicago; John Mackey, founder and CEO of Whole Foods Market; and others, on the purpose of the corporation.[6] Friedman, a Nobel laureate in economics and the author of a famous 1970 *New York Times Magazine* article titled "The Social Responsibility of Business Is to Increase Its Profits," had no patience with capitalists who claimed,

> Business is not concerned "merely" with profit but also with promoting desirable "social" ends; that business has a "social conscience" and takes seriously its responsibilities for providing

employment, eliminating discrimination, avoiding pollution and whatever else may be the catchwords of the contemporary crop of reformers.[7]

He wrote that such people are "preaching pure and unadulterated socialism. Businessmen who talk this way are unwitting puppets of the intellectual forces that have been undermining the basis of a free society these past decades."[8]

Mackey disagreed vehemently with Friedman. A self-described ardent libertarian who likes to quote Ludwig von Mises on Austrian economics and Abraham Maslow on humanistic psychology, and is a student of astrology, Mackey believes Friedman's view of business is too narrow and underestimates the humanitarian potential of capitalism. Selected portions of this debate are reprinted below, beginning with Mackey's passionate, personal vision of the social responsibility of business.

In 1970 Milton Friedman wrote that "there is one and only one social responsibility of business—to use its resources and engage in activities designed to increase its profits so long as it stays within the rules of the game, which is to say, engages in open and free competition without deception or fraud." That's the orthodox view among free market economists: that the only social responsibility a law-abiding business has is to maximize profits for the shareholders.

I strongly disagree. I'm a businessman and a free market libertarian, but I believe that the enlightened corporation should try to create value for *all* of its constituencies. From an investor's perspective, the purpose of the business is to maximize profits. But that's not the purpose for other stakeholders—for customers, employees, suppliers, and the community. Each of those groups will define the purpose of the business in terms of its own needs and desires, and each perspective is valid and legitimate.

Mackey continues,

We have not achieved our tremendous increase in shareholder value by making shareholder value the primary purpose of our business . . . the most successful businesses put the customer first, ahead of the investors. In the profit-centered business, customer happiness is merely a means to an end: maximizing profits. In the customer-centered business, customer happiness is an end in itself, and will be pursued with greater interest, passion, and empathy than the profit-centered business is capable of.

Not surprisingly, Friedman respected Whole Foods' success but took issue with its business philosophy:

> Maximizing profits is an end from the private point of view; it is a means from the social point of view. A system based on private property and free markets is a sophisticated means of enabling people to cooperate in their economic activities without compulsion; it enables separated knowledge to assure that each resource is used for its most valued use, and is combined with other resources in the most efficient way.

Mackey replied,

> While Friedman believes that taking care of customers, employees, and business philanthropy are means to the end of increasing investor profits, I take the exact opposite view: Making high profits is the means to the end of fulfilling Whole Foods' core business mission. We want to improve the health and well-being of everyone on the planet through higher-quality foods and better nutrition, and we can't fulfill this mission unless we are highly profitable. High profits are necessary to fuel our growth across the United States and the world. Just as people cannot live without eating, so a business cannot live without profits. But most people don't live to eat, and neither must a business live just to make profits.

Mackey's logic was perhaps most effectively first articulated by Peter Drucker in 1974 in his famous book *Management: Tasks, Responsibilities and Practices*:

> The purpose of a business is not to make a profit. Profit is a necessity and a social responsibility. A business, regardless of the

economic and legal arrangements of society, must produce enough profit to cover the risks of committing today's economic resources to the uncertainties of the future; to produce the capital for the jobs of tomorrow; and to pay for all the non-economic needs and satisfactions of society from defense and the administration of justice to the schools and the hospitals, and from the museums to the boy scouts. But profit is not the purpose of business. Rather a business exists and gets paid for its economic contribution. Its purpose is to create a customer.[9]

This discussion raises questions that transcend the legal debate on fiduciary obligations. It asks us to consider questions, such as, What does society want from corporations? What are the moral obligations and responsibilities of business? Who has the right to make such decisions in a public company? Is shareholder wealth maximization the right objective? And what obligations does a company have to other stakeholders, such as employees or suppliers, and the community at large? And are these objectives necessarily in conflict with each other? If so, how should trade-offs be made? What is more, the discussion suggests that to be consistent and effective, directors and boards should have ready answers to many, if not all, of the questions and know where they agree or disagree. As we shall see, regrettably, this is not true. Not only has the United States, as a society, changed its perspective on this issue several times, but also, today, the majority of directors remain confused, sometimes intimidated, by the law and often unwilling or unable to debate these issues openly.

The Primacy of Shareholder Interests: A Historical Perspective[10]

During the first part of the 19th century, the corporation was viewed as a social instrument for the state to carry out its public policy goals, and each instance of incorporation required a special act of the state legislature. The function of the law was to protect stakeholders by making sure corporations would not pursue activities beyond their original charter or state of incorporation. By the end of the 19th century, states began to allow general incorporation, which fueled an explosive growth in the creation of companies for private business purposes. In its aftermath, concern for stakeholder welfare gave way to the concept of managing the corporation for shareholders' profits.

In 1919 the primacy of shareholder value maximization was affirmed in a ruling by the Michigan State Supreme Court in *Dodge vs. Ford Motor Company*. Henry Ford wanted to invest Ford Motor Company's considerable retained earnings in the company rather than distribute it to shareholders. The Dodge brothers, minority shareholders in Ford Motor Company, brought suit against Ford, alleging that his intention to benefit employees and consumers was at the expense of shareholders. In their ruling, the Michigan court agreed with the Dodge brothers:

> A business corporation is organized and carried on primarily for the profit of the stockholders. The powers of the directors are to be employed for that end. The discretion of directors is to be exercised in the choice of means to attain that end, and does not extend to a change in the end itself, to the reduction of profits, or to the non-distribution of profits among stockholders in order to devote them to other purposes.[11]

In *The Modern Corporation and Private Property*, published in 1932, Adolph Berle and Gardiner Means provided important intellectual support for the shareholder value norm. In this now classic book, the authors called attention to a new phenomenon affecting corporations in the United States at the time. They noted that ownership of capital had become widely dispersed among many small shareholders, yet control was concentrated in the hands of just a few managers. Berle and Means warned that the separation of ownership and control would destroy the very foundation of the existing economic order and argued that managing on behalf of the shareholders was the *sine qua non* of managerial decision making because shareholders were property owners.

Following the 1929 stock market crash and the Great Depression, stakeholder concerns were being voiced once again. If the corporation is an entity separate from its shareholders, it was argued, it has citizenship responsibilities.[12] According to this point of view, rather than being an agent for shareholders, the role of management is that of a trustee with citizenship responsibilities on behalf of all constituencies, even if it means a reduction in shareholder value. In the following years, states adopted a number of stakeholder statutes reflecting this new sense of corporate responsibility toward nonshareholding constituencies, such as labor, consumers, and the natural environment.

By the end of the 20th century, however, despite state-level legislative efforts to the contrary, American-style market-driven capitalism had prevailed and the pendulum swung back to the shareholder. Friedman's view that the "sole social responsibility of business is to increase profits" energized a push back on corporate social responsibility.[13] In the meantime, agency theory[14] and the concept of the corporation as a nexus of contracts[15] had become influential doctrines in finance and economics.

To protect the interests of other stakeholders, 30 states in the United States enacted stakeholder statutes that allowed directors to consider the interests of nonshareholder constituencies in corporate decisions. Thus, the law gave boards latitude in determining what is in the best long-term interests of the corporation and how to take the interests of other stakeholders into account. Nevertheless, the mainstream of U.S. corporate law remains committed to the principle of shareholder wealth maximization.[16]

Governance Without a Shared Purpose?

The lack of a clear, shared consensus about why a company exists, to whom directors are accountable, and what criteria they should use to make decisions—in the law as well as in society at large—is a significant obstacle to increasing the effectiveness of the corporate governance function. When boards operate with tacit assumptions about their objectives and loyalties, they may hide potential disagreements among their members and sacrifice effectiveness. Such hidden disagreements make it difficult to get consensus on complex issues, such as what qualifications a CEO should have, whether or not to outsource parts of the value chain, or how to evaluate and compensate top management.

Lorsch (1989) first identified the confusion among directors about their accountabilities. Based on their beliefs, he categorized directors as belonging to one of three groups: *traditionalists*, *rationalizers*, or *broad constructionists*.[17] Each has a different vision of what the modern corporation's fundamental purpose is and, therefore, to whom and for what a board should be held accountable.

Traditionalists see themselves as accountable to shareholders only. For them, there is no need to debate the fundamental purpose of the modern corporation—it is and always has been the maximization of shareholder value. They do not believe there is a conflict between putting the shareholder first and responding to the needs of other constituencies, and therefore experience little role ambiguity or conflict. Members of this group find support for their position in a narrow interpretation of current state and federal law. They also tend to view the highly publicized abuses at Enron, WorldCom, Vivendi, and other companies as anomalies made possible by imperfections in the current system rather than as indicators of more systemic problems.

A second, larger group—the *rationalizers*—experiences more anxiety about their role as directors. They recognize that, in today's complex, global economy, real tensions can occur between the interests of different constituencies and that not all decisions can be reduced to the simple "What is good for the shareholder is good for everyone else" formula. Examples include whether or not to close a domestic plant in favor of manufacturing in a low-cost, foreign location; whether or not to outsource production to lower cost suppliers; or how to respond to pressures for "greener" operations. Nevertheless, feeling constrained by the law and guided by the (primarily Delaware) law, that is the way rationalizers behave.

The final group, which Lorsch labels as the *broad constructionists*, recognizes specific responsibilities to constituencies other than shareholders and is willing to act on its convictions. Directors belonging to this group constantly struggle to balance their views with the more traditional view of a director's accountabilities and—to stay within the boundaries of the law—frame their decisions in terms of what is in the best long-term interest of the corporation as a whole.

Lorsch summarized his findings as, "Thus we found the majority of directors felt trapped in a dilemma between their traditional legal responsibility to shareholders, whom they consider too interested in short-term payout, and their beliefs about what is best, in the long run, for the health of the company."[18] He further observed that it appeared that, in many boards, a group norm had evolved, prohibiting open discussion of a board's true purpose and that a lot of directors were unaware of recent rulings in the evolving legal context that grant them the latitude to consider constituencies other than shareholders.

In recent years the issue of a board's primary role and accountability has, if anything, become even more confusing. Despite strong rhetoric from many quarters advocating maximization of shareholder value as a company's primary goal, there is a growing recognition that a company and the board have broader responsibilities. This trend reflects the fact that real—that is, economic and psychological rather than legal—ownership of the corporation is moving from shareholders to employees, customers, and other stakeholders that make up the human capital of the firm.

This has created real problems for directors. As Lorsch notes,

> Boards have a real challenge in deciding to whom they are really responsible and where their commitments ultimately lie. Directors must think about and discuss among themselves the constituencies and the time horizons they have in mind as they think about the board's responsibilities. Many boards have skirted discussion of these complex issues. They seem too abstract, and reaching a consensus among board members about them can take more of that most precious commodity—time—than directors want to devote.[19]

Is Shareholder Value Maximization the Right Objective?

In their widely cited book *The Value Imperative—Managing for Superior Shareholder Returns*, McTaggart, Kontes, and Mankins (1994) write,

> Maximizing shareholder value is not an abstract, shortsighted, impractical, or even, some might think, sinister objective. On the contrary, it is a concrete, future-oriented, pragmatic, and worthy objective, the pursuit of which motivates and enables managers to make substantially better strategic and organizational decisions than they would in pursuit of any other goal. And its accomplishment is essential to the welfare of all the company's stakeholders, for it is only when wealth is created that customers will continue to

enjoy a flow of new, better, and cheaper products and the world's economies will see new jobs created and old ones improved.[20]

Implicit in this statement are three important assumptions, all of which can be challenged:

1. Shareholder value is the best measure of wealth creation for the firm.
2. Shareholder value maximization produces the greatest competitiveness.
3. Shareholder value maximization fairly serves the interests of the company's other stakeholders.

With respect to the first assumption, it can be argued that "firm value," which also includes the values to all other financial claimants, such as creditors, debt holders, and preferred shareholders, is a better indicator of wealth. The importance of distinguishing between firm value and shareholder value lies in the fact that managers and boards can make decisions that transfer value from debt holders to shareholders and decrease total firm and social value while increasing shareholder value.

The second assumption—that shareholder value maximization produces the greatest long-term competitiveness—can also be challenged. An increasingly influential group of critics, which also includes a substantial number of CEOs, thinks product-market rather than capital-market objectives should guide corporate decision making. They worry that companies that adopt shareholder value maximization as their primary purpose lose sight of producing or delivering a product or service as their central mission and that shareholder value maximization creates a gap between the mission of the corporation and the motivations, desires, and capabilities of the company's employees who only have direct control over real, current, corporate performance. They note that shareholder value maximization is simply not inspiring for employees, even though they often share in some of the gains through benefit, bonus, or option plans. To many of them, shareholders are nameless and faceless, under no obligation to hold their shares for any length of time, never satisfied, and always asking, "What will you do for me next?" Worse, they say, not only does shareholder-value appreciation fail to inspire employees, it may encourage them to view maximizing one's financial well-being as a legitimate or even the only goal. Instead, they want companies to create a moral purpose that not only provides a clear focus on creating competitive advantage for the company but also unites its purpose, strategy, goals, and shared values into one overall, coherent management framework that has the power to motivate constituents and the legitimacy of the corporation's actions in society.[21]

The third assumption—that shareholder maximization is congruent with fairly serving the interests is the firm's other stakeholders—is perhaps most controversial. Proponents of shareholder value maximization—including many economists and finance theorists—are adamant that maximizing shareholder value is not only superior as a fiduciary standard or management objective but also as a societal norm. Jensen (2001), for example, writes,

> Two-hundred years of research in economics and finance have produced the result that if our objective is to maximize the efficiency with which society utilizes its resources (that is to avoid waste and to maximize the size of the pie), then the proper and unique objective for each company in the society is to maximize the long-run total value of the firm. Firm value will not be maximized, of course, with unhappy customers and employees or with poor products. Therefore, consistent with "stakeholder theory" value-maximizing firms will be concerned about relations with all their constituencies. A firm cannot maximize value if it ignores the interest of its stakeholders.[22]

McTaggart et al. (1994) also believe shareholder value maximization allows managers and boards to resolve any conflicts to everyone's long-term benefit. Consider, for example, their prescription for resolving trade-offs between customer- and shareholder-focused investments:

> As long as management invests in higher levels of customer satisfaction that will enable shareholders to earn an adequate return on their investment, there is no conflict between maximizing shareholder value and maximizing customer satisfaction. If, however,

there is insufficient financial benefit to shareholders from attempts to increase customer satisfaction, the conflict should be resolved for the benefit of shareholders to avoid diminishing both the financial health and long-term competitiveness of the business.[23]

Not surprisingly, stakeholder theorists take a different point of view. They argue that shareholders are but one of a number of important stakeholder groups and that, like customers, suppliers, employees, and local communities, shareholders have a stake in and are affected by the firm's success or failure. To stakeholder theory advocates, an exclusive focus on maximizing stockholder wealth is both unwise and ethically wrong; instead, the firm and its managers have special obligations to ensure that the shareholders receive a "fair" return on their investment, but the firm also has special obligations to other stakeholders, which go above and beyond those required by law.[24]

More recently, Ian Davis, managing director of McKinsey, criticized the shareholder value maximization doctrine on altogether different grounds. He observed that, in today's global business environment, the concept of shareholder value is rapidly losing relevance in the face of the larger role played by government and society in shaping business and industry elsewhere in the world:

> In much of the world, government, labor and other social forces have a greater impact on business than in the U.S. or other more free-market Western societies. In China, for example, government is often an owner. If you're talking in China about shareholder value, you will get blank looks. Maximization of shareholder value is in danger of becoming irrelevant.[25]

Finally, a growing number, including CEOs, while not questioning that shareholder value maximization is the right objective, are concerned about its implementation. They worry that the stock market has a bias toward short-term results and that stock price, the most common gauge of shareholder wealth, does not reflect the true long-term value of a company. Lucent Technologies CEO Henry Schacht, for example, has stated, "What has happened to us is that our execution and processes have broken down under the white hot heat of driving for quarterly revenue growth."[26]

Stakeholder Theory: A Viable Alternative?

Although the recognition of stakeholder obligations has been with us since the birth of the modern corporate form, the development of a coherent stakeholder theory awaited a shift in legal thinking from a perspective on shareholders as "owners" to one of "investors," more on a par with providers of other inputs that a company needs to produce goods or services.[27] Whereas the ownership perspective, rooted in property law, provides a natural basis for the primacy of shareholder rights, the view of the corporation as a bundle of contracts permits a different view of the fiduciary obligations of corporate managers. Freeman and McVea (2001) describe stakeholder management as follows:

> The stakeholder framework does not rely on a single overriding management objective for all decisions. As such it provides no rival to the traditional aim of "maximizing shareholder wealth." To the contrary, a stakeholder approach rejects the very idea of maximizing a single-objective function as a useful way of thinking about management strategy. Rather, stakeholder management is a never ending task of balancing and integrating multiple relationships and multiple objectives.[28]

To pragmatists, the rejection of a single criterion for making corporate decisions is problematic. Directors occasionally face situations in which it is impossible to advance the interests of one set of stakeholders and simultaneously protect those of others. Whose interests should they pursue when there is an irreconcilable conflict? Consider the decision whether or not to close down an obsolete plant. The closing will harm the plant's workers and the local community but will benefit shareholders, creditors, employees working at a more modern plant to which the work previously performed at the old plant is transferred, and communities around the modern plant. Without a single guiding decision criterion, how should the board decide?

The problem is not just one of uncertainty or unpredictability. Ultimately, the stakeholder model is flawed because of its failure to account adequately for what Bainbridge (1994) calls "managerial sin."[29] The absence of a single decision-making criterion allows management to freely pursue its own self-interest by playing shareholders off against nonshareholders. When management's interests coincide with those of shareholders, management can justify its decision by saying that shareholder interests prevailed in this instance, and vice versa. The plant closing decision described above provides a useful example: Shareholders and some nonshareholder constituents benefit if the plant is closed, but other nonshareholder constituents lose. If management's compensation is tied to firm size, we can expect it to resist any downsizing of the firm. The plant likely will stay open, with the decision being justified by the impact of a closing on the plant's workers and the local community. In contrast, if management's compensation is linked to firm profitability, the plant will likely close, with the decision being justified by management's concern for the firm's shareholders, creditors, and other constituencies that benefit from the closure decision.

It has been argued that shareholders, in fact, are more vulnerable to management misconduct than nonshareholder constituencies. Legally, shareholders have essentially no power to initiate corporate action and, moreover, are entitled to vote on only very few corporate actions.[30] Rather, formal decision-making power resides mainly with the board of directors.[31] In effect, shareholders, just like nonshareholder constituencies, have but a single mechanism by which they can "negotiate" with management: withholding their inputs (capital). But withholding inputs may be a more effective tool for nonshareholders than it is for shareholders. Some firms go for years without seeking equity investments. If the management groups in these firms disregard shareholder interests, the shareholders have no option other than to sell out at prices that will reflect management's lack of concern for shareholder wealth. In contrast, few firms can survive for long without regular infusions of new employees and new debt financing. As a result, few management groups can prosper while ignoring nonshareholder interests. Nonshareholder constituencies often also are more effective in protecting themselves through the political process. Shareholders—especially individuals—typically have no meaningful political voice. In contrast, many nonshareholder constituencies are represented by cohesive, politically powerful interest groups. Unions, for example, played a major role in passing state antitakeover laws. Environmental concerns are increasingly a factor in regulatory actions. From this point of view, it can be argued that an explicit focus on balancing stakeholder interests is not only impractical but also unnecessary because nonshareholder constituencies already have adequate mechanisms to protect themselves from management misconduct.

Resolving the Conflict: Toward Enlightened Value Maximization?

Jensen believes the inherent conflict between the doctrine of shareholder value maximization and the objectives of stakeholder theory can be resolved by melding together "enlightened" versions of these two philosophies:

> Enlightened value maximization recognizes that communication with and motivation of an organization's managers, employees, and partners is extremely difficult. What this means in practice is that if we simply tell all participants in an organization that its sole purpose is to maximize value, we will not get maximum value for the organization. Value maximization is not a vision or a strategy or even a purpose; it is the scorecard for the organization. We must give people enough structure to understand what maximizing value means so that they can be guided by it and therefore have a chance to actually achieve it. They must be turned on by the vision or the strategy in the sense that it taps into some human desire or passion of their own—for example, a desire to build the world's best automobile or to create a film or play that will move people for centuries. All this can be not only consistent with value seeking, but a major contributor to it.[32]

And,

> Indeed, it is a basic principle of enlightened value maximization that *we cannot maximize the long-term market value of an*

organization if we ignore or mistreat any important constituency.
We cannot create value without good relations with customers,
employees, financial backers, suppliers, regulators, and communities. But having said that, we can now use the value criterion
for choosing among those competing interests. I say "competing"
interests because no constituency can be given full satisfaction if
the firm is to flourish and survive. Moreover, we can be sure—
again, apart from the possibility of externalities and monopoly
power—that using this value criterion will result in making society as well off as it can be.[33]

Thus, Jensen defines "enlightened" stakeholder theory simply as stakeholder theory with the specification that maximizing the firm's total long-
term market value is the right objective function. The words "long-term"
are key here. As Jensen notes,

In this way, enlightened stakeholder theorists can see that although
stockholders are not some special constituency that ranks above all
others, long-term stock value is an important determinant (along
with the value of debt and other instruments) of total long-term
firm value. They would recognize that value creation gives management a way to assess the tradeoffs that must be made among
competing constituencies, and that it allows for principled decision making independent of the personal preferences of managers
and directors.[34]

Even though shareholder value maximization is increasingly being challenged on pragmatic as well as moral grounds, its roots in private property
law, however—a profound element in the American ethos—guarantee
that it will continue to dominate the U.S. approach to corporate law for
the foreseeable future. As a practical matter, the courts have given boards
increasing latitude in determining what is in the best long-term interests
of the corporation and how to take the interests of other stakeholders
into account. This latitude makes it imperative that directors openly and
fully discuss these issues and agree on a clear, unambiguous statement of
purpose for the corporation.

CHAPTER 3

The Board of Directors

Role and Composition

The Board's Responsibilities: The Legal Framework

From a legal perspective, the board of a public corporation is charged with setting a corporation's policy and direction, electing and appointing officers and agents to act on behalf of the corporation, and acting on other major matters affecting the corporation. In this context, individual directors' duties and responsibilities are described in the American Bar Association's *Corporate Director's Guidebook, Fourth Edition* (2004) with language, such as the following:

- *in good faith.* Acting honestly and dealing fairly. In contrast, a lack of good faith would be evidenced by acting, or causing the corporation to act, for the director's personal benefit or for some purpose other than to advance the welfare of the corporation and its economic interests and may also include acting on a corporate matter without making a reasonable effort to be appropriately informed.
- *reasonably believes.* Although the director's honest belief is subjective, the qualification that it must be reasonable (i.e., based upon a rational analysis of the situation understandable to others) makes the standard of conduct also objective, not just subjective.
- *best interests of the corporation.* Emphasizing the director's primary allegiance to the corporate entity.

- *care.* Expressing the need to pay attention, to ask questions, to act diligently to become and remain generally informed, and, when appropriate, to bring relevant information to the attention of the other directors. In particular, these activities include reading materials and engaging in other preparation in advance of meetings, asking questions of management until satisfied that all information significant to a decision is available to the board and has been considered, and requesting legal or other expert advice when appropriate to a board decision.
- *person in a like position.* Avoiding the implication of special qualifications and incorporating the basic attributes of common sense, practical wisdom, and informed judgment generally associated with the position of corporate director.
- *under similar circumstances.* Recognizing that the nature and extent of the preparation for and deliberations leading up to decision making and the level of oversight will vary, depending on the corporation concerned, its particular situation, and the nature of the decision to be made.[1]

This language provides guidance about how directors should comply with the underlying duty of care, the business judgment rule, and the duty of loyalty, briefly introduced in chapter 2, which I restate here more formally:[2]

- *Duty of Care.* The Duty of Care is the most important duty owed by a director to a corporation. A typical (state) corporation statute defining a director's Duty of Care provides that a director's duties must be performed "with such care, including reasonable inquiry, as an ordinarily prudent person in a like position would use under similar circumstances." This Duty of Care is very broad and requires directors to diligently perform their obligations.
- *Business Judgment Rule.* The Business Judgment Rule works in conjunction with the director's Duty of Care. Under this rule, a director will not be held liable for mere negligence if exercising his or her Duty of Care. The rule can be stated as, "A

director who exercises reasonable diligence and who, in good faith, makes an honest, unbiased decision will not be held liable for mere mistakes and errors in business judgment." The rule protects directors from decisions that turn out badly for their corporation, even when the directors acted diligently and in good faith in authorizing the decision.

- *Duty of Loyalty.* The Duty of Loyalty exists as a result of the fiduciary relationship between directors and the corporation. A fiduciary relationship is defined as a relationship of trust and confidence, such as between a doctor and patient, or attorney and client. The nature of the relationship includes the concepts that neither party may take selfish advantage of the other's trust and may not deal with the subject of the relationship in a way that benefits one party to the disadvantage of the other. A director must perform his or her duties in good faith and in a manner in which the director believes is in the best interests of the corporation and its shareholders. Essentially, this duty means that while serving a corporation, the director must give the corporation the first opportunity to take advantage of any business opportunities that he or she becomes aware of and that are within the scope of the corporation's business. If the board of directors chooses not to take advantage of a business opportunity brought to its attention by a director, the director may then go forward without violating his or her duty.

Liability can exist for officers and directors when they cause financial harm to the corporation, act solely on their own behalf and to the detriment of the corporation, or commit a crime or wrongful act. Certain acts may subject an officer or director to personal liability, and other acts, although they would otherwise subject them to liability, may be either indemnified by or insured against by the corporation.[3]

A Board's Role: A Governance Perspective

What does the phrase "direct the affairs of the company" really mean? To provide greater clarity, numerous individuals and organizations have developed more specific descriptions in recent years. One frequently cited description was developed by the Business Roundtable:

- First, the paramount duty of the board of directors of a public corporation is to select the chief executive officer (CEO) and to oversee the CEO and senior management in the competent and ethical operation of the corporation on a day-to-day basis
- Second, it is the responsibility of management to operate the corporation in an effective and ethical manner to produce value for shareholders. Senior management is expected to know how the corporation earns its income and what risks the corporation is undertaking in the course of carrying out its business. The CEO and board of directors should set a "tone at the top" that establishes a culture of legal compliance and integrity. Management and directors should never put personal interests ahead of or in conflict with the interests of the corporation
- Third, it is the responsibility of management, under the oversight of the audit committee and the board, to produce financial statements that fairly present the financial condition and results of operations of the corporation and to make the timely disclosures investors need to assess the financial and business soundness and risks of the corporation
- Fourth, it is the responsibility of the board, through its audit committee, to engage an independent accounting firm to audit the financial statements prepared by management, issue an opinion that those statements are fairly stated in accordance with Generally Accepted Accounting Principles and oversee the corporation's relationship with the outside auditor
- Fifth, it is the responsibility of the board, through its corporate governance committee, to play a leadership role in shaping the corporate governance of the corporation. The corporate governance committee also should select and recommend to the board qualified director candidates for election by the corporation's shareholders
- Sixth, it is the responsibility of the board, through its compensation committee, to adopt and oversee the implementation of

compensation policies, establish goals for performance-based compensation, and determine the compensation of the CEO and senior management

- Seventh, it is the responsibility of the board to respond appropriately to shareholders' concerns
- Eighth, it is the responsibility of the corporation to deal with its employees, customers, suppliers and other constituencies in a fair and equitable manner.[4]

Milstein, Gregory, and Grapsas (2006) take a somewhat broader perspective. First, they note, the board needs to take charge of its own focus, agenda, and information flow. This enables a board to provide management with meaningful guidance and support. It also helps the board focus its attention appropriately, determine its own agenda, and obtain the information it needs to make objective judgments. Second, the board must ensure that management not only performs but performs with integrity. Selecting, monitoring, and compensating management and, when necessary, replacing management, therefore continue to lie at the heart of board activity. Third, the board must set expectations about the tone and culture of the company. The standards of ethics and business conduct that are followed—or not followed—throughout a company impact the bottom line in many ways. "Tone at the top" should be a priority throughout the company and not viewed simply as a compliance matter. Fourth, the board should work with management to formulate corporate strategy. After agreeing to a strategic course with management through an iterative process, the board should determine the benchmarks that will evidence success or failure in achieving strategic objectives and then regularly monitor performance against those objectives. Fifth, it is the board's duty to ensure that the corporate culture, the agreed strategy, management incentive compensation, and the company's approach to audit and accounting, internal controls, and disclosure are consistent and aligned. And sixth, it is the board's duty to help management understand the expectations of shareholders and regulators. Boards can help management recognize that shareholders have a legitimate interest in more meaningful input into the board selection process, in terms of both nominating procedures and voting methods. Similarly, boards can help management recognize and address the concerns that excessive compensation raises among shareholders, regulators, rating agencies, and others.[5]

Both descriptions are useful for developing a basic understanding of a board's responsibilities. In broad terms, they fall into three categories: (a) to make decisions, (b) to monitor corporate activity, and (c) to advise management. The key issue here is deciding which board posture is appropriate at what time. While the law, corporate bylaws, and other documents frame many of the decisions a board must make, such as appointing a CEO or approving the financials, they do not provide much guidance with respect to the most important decision a board must make—when must board oversight become active intervention? For example, when should a board step in and remove the current CEO? When should directors veto a major capital appropriation or strategic move?

Lists never can fully capture the complexity and intricacies of the governance function because they do not consider the specific challenges associated with different governance scenarios. In particular, the precise role of a board will vary depending on the nature of the company, industry, and competitive situation and the presence or absence of special circumstances, such as a hostile takeover bid or a corporate crisis, among other factors.

The Nature of the Company, Industry, and Competitive Situation

It seems self-evident that a board's role depends largely on the nature and the strategic challenges of the company and the industry. The challenges faced by small, private, or closely held companies are not the same as those of larger, public corporations. In addition to their traditional fiduciary role, directors in small companies often are key advisers in strategic planning, raising, and allocating capital, human resources planning, and sometimes even performance appraisal. In large public corporations, directors are focused more on exercising oversight than on planning, on capital allocation and control rather than on the raising of capital, and on management development and succession activities rather than on broader human resources responsibilities.

Public company ownership patterns are not homogeneous either, and different ownership structures may call for different governance approaches. The first, and most common, board situation is one in which a corporation has no controlling shareholder. In that case, directors should behave as if there is a single absentee owner whose long-term interests they serve. A primary responsibility for the board in this scenario is to appoint and, if necessary, change management, just as an intelligent owner would do if he were present. Commenting on individual director's responsibilities in these circumstances, Buffett (1993) writes,

> In this plain-vanilla case, a director who sees something he doesn't like should attempt to persuade the other directors of his views. If he is successful, the board will have the muscle to make the appropriate change. Suppose, though, that the unhappy director can't get other directors to agree with him. He should then feel free to make his views known to the absentee owners. Directors seldom do that, of course. The temperament of many directors would in fact be incompatible with critical behavior of that sort. But I see nothing improper in such actions, assuming the issues are serious. Naturally, the complaining director can expect a vigorous rebuttal from the unpersuaded directors, a prospect that should discourage the dissenter from pursuing trivial or non-rational causes.[6]

The second situation occurs when the controlling owner is also the manager. At some companies, such as Google, this arrangement is facilitated by the existence of two classes of stock endowed with disproportionate voting power. In these situations, the board does not act as an agent between owners and management, and directors cannot affect change except through persuasion. Therefore, if the owner or manager is mediocre—or worse, is overreaching—there is little a director can do about it except object. And if there is no change and the matter is sufficiently serious, the outside directors should resign. Their resignation will signal their doubts about management, and it will emphasize that no outsider is in a position to correct the owner or manager's shortcomings.[7]

The third public corporation governance situation occurs when there is a controlling owner who is not involved in management. This case, examples of which are Hershey Foods and Dow Jones, puts the outside directors in a potentially value-creating position. If they become unhappy with either the competence or integrity of the manager, they can go directly to the owner (who may also be on the board) and make their views known. This situation helps an outside director, since he need make his case only to a single, presumably interested owner who can immediately make a change if the argument is persuasive. Even so, the dissatisfied director has only that single course of action. If he remains unsatisfied about a critical matter, he has no choice but to resign.[8]

It will also be readily apparent that the role of the board will vary depending on the size of the company, the industries it serves, and the competitive challenges it faces. Global corporations face different challenges from domestic ones; the issues in regulated industries are different from those in technology or service industries, and high growth scenarios make different demands on boards than more mature ones. Finally, in times of turbulence or rapid change in the industry, boards often are called on to play a more active, strategic role than in calmer times. Special events or opportunities, such as takeovers, mergers, and acquisitions, fall into this category.

The Presence or Absence of Special Circumstances, Such as a Hostile Takeover Bid or a Corporate Crisis

Company crises can take on many different forms—defective products, hostile takeovers, executive misconduct, natural disasters that threaten operations, and many more. But, as boards know very well, they all have one thing in common: They threaten the stock price and sometimes the continued existence of the company. Some examples follow:

- In June 2008, with encouragement from federal regulators, JP Morgan executed a takeover bid for Wall Street giant Bear Stearns to prevent the bank's collapse as a consequence of the U.S. mortgage debt crisis. The $240 million acquisition price represented a substantial discount on its share price at the end of trading the week before, which valued the bank at around $3.5 billion.

- In 2002, when allegations of insider trading against Martha Stewart were reported, the stock price of Martha Stewart Omnimedia fell some 40% in just 3 weeks.
- In 1993, an allegation of *E. coli* contamination in the beef served by the Jack in the Box hamburger chain caused the company's share price to plummet from $14 to about $3 in a matter of hours.
- In 1985, A. H. Robins, the maker of the Dalkon Shield, an intrauterine device, was forced to declare bankruptcy, after collapsing under a wave of personal injury lawsuits.

As these examples attest, there are few situations in which directors' fiduciary duties to shareholders are so clearly on view as in times of crisis.[9]

The Board's Role: Governance, Not Management

Beyond implementing reforms and best practices, boards are being counseled to become more involved.[10] Rubber-stamping decisions, populating boards with friends of the CEO, and convening board meetings on the golf course are out; engagement, transparency, independence, knowing the company inside and out, and adding value are in. This all sounds good. There is a real danger, however, that the rise in shareholder activism, the new regulatory environment, and related social factors are pushing boards toward micromanagement and meddling.

This issue is troubling, and clear evidence that the important differences that separate *governance from management*—critical to effective governance—are still not sufficiently well understood by directors, executives, regulators, and the popular press alike. And regrettably, faced with the need to be more involved, the most obvious opportunity (and danger) is for boards to expand their involvement into—or, more accurately, intrude into—management's territory.

The key issues are how and to whom boards add value.[11] Specifically, the potential of directors to add value is all too often framed in terms of their ability to add value to management by giving advice on issues such as strategy, choice of markets, and other factors of corporate success. While this may be valuable, *it obscures the primary role of the board to govern, the purpose of which is to add value to shareholders and other stakeholders.* John Carver, well-known governance consultant and author, does not mince words:

> Governance is an extension of ownership, not of operations. Directors must be more allied with shareholders than with managers. Their mentality, their language, their concerns, their skills, their choice of interactions are subsets of ownership, not of management. As long as we view governance as übermanagement—focusing on management methods, strategies and planning—finding a new balance between micromanagement and detachment . . . will be hard to come by.[12]

A greater arms-length relationship between management and the board, therefore, is both desirable and unavoidable. Recent governance reforms focused on creating greater independence and minimizing managerial excess while enhancing executive accountability have already created greater tension in the relationship between management and the board. The Sarbanes-Oxley Act, for example, effectively asks boards to substitute verification for trust. Section 404 of the act requires management at all levels to "sign off" on key financial statements.

This is not necessarily bad because trust and verification are not necessarily incompatible. In fact, we need both. But we should also realize that effective governance is about striking a reasonable accommodation between verification and trust—not about elevating one over the other. The history of human nature shows that adversarial relationships can create their own pathologies of miscommunication and mismanaged expectations with respect to risk and reward. This makes defining the trade-offs that shape effective governance so difficult. Is better governance defined primarily by the active prevention of abuse? Or by the active promotion of risk taking and profitability? The quick and easy answer is that it should mean all of those things. However, as recurrent crises in corporate governance around the world have shown, it is hard to do even one of those things consistently well. What is more, a board trying to do all of these things well is not merely an active board; it is a board actively running the company. This is not overseeing management or holding management accountable—it *is* management. Therefore, the corporate governance reform agenda risks becoming an initiative that effectively dissolves most of the critical, traditional distinctions between the chief executive and the board.[13]

Governance Guidelines

As part of the recent wave of governance reforms, the NYSE adopted new rules that require companies to adopt and publicly disclose their corporate governance policies. Specifically, the following subjects must be addressed in the guidelines:

- *Director qualification standards.* These standards, in addition to requiring independence, may also address other substantive qualification requirements, including policies limiting the number of boards on which a director may sit and director tenure, retirement, and succession.
- *Director responsibilities.* These responsibilities should clearly articulate what is expected from a director, including basic duties and responsibilities with respect to attendance at board meetings and advance review of meeting materials.
- *Director access to management and, as necessary and appropriate, to an independent advisor.* Clear policies should be adopted that define protocols for director access to corporate managers and identify situations when the board should retain external advisors.
- *Director compensation.* Director compensation guidelines should include general principles for determining the form and amount of director compensation (and for reviewing those principles, as appropriate).
- *Director orientation and continuing education.* Director orientation and continuing education should be the responsibility of the governance committee, if one exists. If the board does not have a separate governance committee, the full board, the nominating committee, or both, should have this responsibility.

- *Management succession.* Succession planning should include policies and principles for CEO selection and performance review, as well as policies regarding succession in the event of an emergency or the retirement of the CEO.
- *Annual performance evaluation of the board.* The board should conduct a self-evaluation at least annually to determine whether it and its committees and their individual directors are functioning effectively.

Best practice suggests that the board should review the guidelines at least annually. By elaborating on the board's and directors' basic duties, a carefully constructed set of governance guidelines will help both the board and individual directors understand their obligations and the general boundaries within which they will operate.

Recent Board Trends[14]

Board Size

The optimal size of a board has been the subject of much debate in recent years. As a general proposition, smaller boards have a number of advantages over larger ones: They are easier to convene, require less effort to lead, and often have a more relaxed, informal culture. Research on group decision making supports the contention that smaller groups typically are more effective.

As a practical matter, however, board size should be governed by the skills needed to do the job. Larger corporations with more complex structures, substantial global interests, or multibusiness operations will require larger boards than smaller, mainly domestic, single-business firms. Today, the average Standard & Poor's 500 board has 11 directors, compared to 18 directors about 25 years ago. It is unlikely boards will shrink further, however, as a result of new rules and proposals requiring that the audit, nominating or governance, and compensation committees of boards in publicly held companies be composed of independent directors only, in some cases, with specialized expertise (audit committee).

Board Membership

Fewer CEOs are accepting directorships, for two reasons. First, many boards—in the wake of the recent scandals and the Sarbanes-Oxley legislation—now insist that the chief executive concentrate fully on his or her job and restrict the number of outside boards the CEO can serve or, in some cases, prohibit it altogether. Second, as boards expand their role to areas, such as company strategy, they look for directors who have risen through specific functional areas in which the company must excel in order to compete effectively—sales and marketing, global operations, manufacturing, and others. And, in the aftermath of Sarbanes-Oxley, directors with a background in finance, especially chief financial officers (CFOs), are in strong demand.[15]

For a while, it looked as though the reduced availability of CEOs and the growing demand for specialized directors would significantly reduce the talent pool of qualified directors and make it even more difficult for companies to attract new board members. Fortunately, this has not proven to be the case. If anything, the talent pool has become larger as boards are changing the definition of what constitutes a qualified candidate and widening their search. Instead of focusing almost exclusively on CEOs as candidates for the board, companies are increasingly tapping division presidents and other executives who have experience running large operations or bring specialist expertise. The redefinition of director qualifications has also expanded the talent pool of diversity candidates who may not have risen to chief executive but excel in a critical, functional area.

These changes do not mean that attracting qualified directors has become easier. Although the pool of qualified candidates is larger, many candidates are far more reluctant to serve. More than ever, candidates perform extensive due diligence about the companies recruiting them and look for ways to mitigate as much as possible the risk of associating themselves with a disaster or incurring personal liability. They are also far more critical and objective about their ability to add value, particularly in complex organizations, such as conglomerates, or industries like financial services and insurance. The overwhelming reason why candidates decline to serve, however, remains a lack of time. Given their already enormous responsibilities, many qualified and desirable director candidates feel that they will be unable to devote adequate attention to the job.

Director Independence

The proposition that boards should "act independently of management, through a thoughtful and diligent decision-making process," has been a major focus of corporate governance reform in recent years.[16] In the United States, the Sarbanes-Oxley Act of 2002, as well as the revised NYSE and NASDAQ listing rules, as affirmed by the SEC, are premised on a belief that director independence is essential to effective corporate governance. In the United Kingdom, the Cadbury Commission's report of 1990—The Code of Best Practice—included a recommendation for having at least three nonexecutive directors on the board. Currently, reflecting this broad consensus, about 10 out of the average 12 directors of a major U.S. public company board are nonexecutives; in the United Kingdom, the corresponding number is a little less than half.

The idea of an independent board is intuitively appealing. Director independence, defined as the absence of any conflicts of interest through personal or professional ties with the corporation or its management, suggests objectivity and a capacity to be impartial and decisive and therefore a stronger fiduciary. At times a board needs to discuss issues that involve some or all of the company's senior executives; this is difficult to do with senior executives on the board. The independence requirement also stops destructive practices, such as "rewarding" former CEOs for their accomplishments by giving them a role on the board. Having the former CEO on the board almost always limits the ability of the new CEO to develop his or her own relationship with the board and put his or her imprint on the organization. There is also limited evidence that outsider-dominated boards are more proactive in firing underperforming CEOs and less willing to go along with outsized compensation proposals or vote for poison pills.

Director independence should not be viewed as a proxy for good governance, however. At times, not having more insiders on the board actually can reduce a board's effectiveness as an oversight body or as counsel to the CEO. Independent, nonexecutive directors can never be as knowledgeable about a company's business as executive directors or senior managers. CEOs say that some of their most valuable directors are those with experience in the same industry, counter to current independence tests. The higher the proportion of outside directors, therefore, the more difficult it is to foster high-quality, deep board deliberations. Moreover, it is less likely that a CEO can mislead a board, intentionally or otherwise, when some of the directors are insiders who also have intimate knowledge of the company.[17] Boards mostly comprised of independent directors must, at a minimum, therefore, create regular opportunities to interact with senior executives other than the CEO. The more complex a company's business is, the more important such communications are.

The bottom line is that effective corporate governance does not depend on the independence of some particular subset of directors but *on the independent behavior of the board as a whole.* The focus should be on fostering *board independence* as a *behavioral* norm, a psychological quality, rather than on quasi-legal definitions of director independence. Director independence can contribute to but is no guarantee for better governance.

Board Leadership: Should We Separate the Chairman and CEO Positions?

Few issues in corporate governance are as contentious as the question of whether the roles of chairman and CEO should be separated or combined. In the United Kingdom, about 95% of all Financial Times Stock Exchange (FTSE) 350 companies adhere to the principle that different people should hold each of these roles. In the United States, by contrast, most companies still combine them, although the idea of splitting the two roles is gaining momentum. In the last 2 years, Boeing, Dell, the Walt Disney Company, MCI, Oracle, and Tenet Healthcare all have done so, and a new study finds that roughly one third of U.S. companies have adopted such a split-leadership structure, up from a historical level of about one fifth.[18]

Arguments for splitting the two roles, emanating chiefly from the United Kingdom—and other countries that overwhelmingly embrace the idea of separate roles (particularly Germany, the Netherlands, South Africa, Australia, and, to a lesser extent, Canada)—reflect four schools of thought.[19]

The first is that the separation of the chairman and CEO positions is a key component of board independence because of the fundamental differences and potential conflicts between these roles. The CEO runs the company—the argument goes—and the chairman runs the board, one of whose responsibilities it is to monitor the CEO. If the chairman and the CEO are one and the same, it is hard for the board to criticize the CEO or to express independent opinions. A separate chairman, responsible for setting the board's agenda, is more likely to probe and encourage debate at board meetings. Separating the two roles is, therefore, essentially a check on the CEO's power.

A second argument is that a nonexecutive chairman can serve as a valuable sounding board, mentor, and advocate to the CEO. Proponents of this view note that CEOs today face enough challenges without having to run the board and that a relationship with the chairman based on mutual trust and regular contact is good for the CEO, shareholders, and the company. For this to happen, however, it is essential that, from the outset, the two roles be clearly defined to avoid territorial disputes or misunderstandings.

A third reason for supporting the two-role model is that a nonexecutive chairman is ideally placed to assess the CEO's performance, taking into account the views of fellow board directors. Advocates maintain that the presence of a separate, independent chairman can help maintain a longer term perspective and reduce the risk that the CEO will focus too much on shorter term goals, especially when there are powerful incentives and rewards to do so. They add that he is also in a good position to play a helpful role in succession planning. And when a CEO departs, voluntarily or otherwise, the chairman's continued presence in charge of the board can reduce the level of trauma in the business and the investor community.

A fourth and final argument concerns the time needed to do both jobs and do them well. It can be argued that as companies grow more complex, a strong board is more vital than ever to the health of the company, and this requires a skilled chairman who is not distracted by the daily pull of the business and can devote the required time and energy. This may take one or more days per week and involve such tasks as maintaining contact with directors between meetings, organizing board evaluations, listening to shareholder concerns, acting as an ambassador for the company, and liaising with regulators, thereby allowing the CEO to concentrate on running the business.

Although these arguments increasingly resonate with U.S. directors and shareholders, many CEOs resist the change. Why, they ask, should corporate wrongdoing at a small number of S&P 500 companies be a compelling reason for changing a system that has worked well for so long? Moral and ethical failures are part of the human condition, they note, and no rules or regulations can guarantee the honesty of a leader. Some allow that, at times, a temporary split in roles may be desirable or necessary—when a company is experiencing a crisis, for example, or when a new CEO is appointed who lacks governance and boardroom experience. But they maintain that such instances are infrequent and temporary and do not justify sweeping change. Overall, they argue, the combined model has served the U.S. economy well, and splitting the roles might set up two power centers, which would impair decision making.

Critics of the split-role model also point out that finding the right chairman is difficult and that what works in the United Kingdom does not necessarily work in the United States. Executives in the United Kingdom tend to retire earlier and tend to view the nonexecutive chairman role (often a 6-year commitment) as the pinnacle of a business career. This is not the case in the United States, where the normal retirement age is higher.

To allay concerns that combined leadership compromises a board's independence, opponents of separation have proposed the idea of a "lead director": a nonexecutive who acts as a link between the chairman–CEO and the outside directors, consults with the chairman–CEO on the agenda of board meetings and performs other independence-enhancing functions. Some 30% of the largest U.S. companies have taken this approach. Its defenders claim that—combined with other measures, such as requiring a majority of independent directors and board meetings without the presence of management—this alternative obviates the need for a separate chairman.

On balance, the arguments for separating the roles of chairman and CEO are persuasive because separation gives boards a structural basis for acting independently. And reducing the power of the CEO in the process may not be bad; compared with other leading Western economies, the United States concentrates corporate authority in a single person to an unusual extent.[20] Furthermore, rather than create confusion about accountability, the separation of roles makes it clear that the board's principal function is to govern—that is, to oversee the company's management, and hence to protect the shareholders' interests—while the CEO's function is to manage the company well.

Separating the two roles, of course, is no guarantee for board effectiveness. A structurally independent board will not necessarily exercise that independence: Some companies with a separate chairman and CEO have failed miserably in carrying out their oversight functions. What is more, a chairman without a strong commitment to the job can stand in the way of board effectiveness. The separation of roles must therefore be complemented by the right boardroom culture and by a sound process for selecting the chairman. The challenge of finding the right nonexecutive chairman who must not only have the experience, personality, and leadership skills to mesh with the current board and management but also must show that the board is not a rubber stamp for the CEO, should not be underestimated. The ideal candidate must have enough time to devote to the job, strong interpersonal skills, a working knowledge of the industry, and a willingness to play a behind-the-scenes role. The best candidate is often an independent director who has served on the board for several years.

Board Committees and Director Compensation

A greater and more effective use of committees also stands out as one of the key changes in board functioning over the last 50 years. Committees permit the board to divide up its work among the directors; they also allow board members to develop specialized knowledge about specific issues. The value of having standing committees has been recognized by the NYSE, the NASDAQ, and the Securities and Exchange Commission (SEC), and today public company boards are required to have independent *audit, nominating (and governance)*, and *compensation* committees. In addition, a growing number of companies are creating board committees to better communicate with and stay abreast of the concerns of external stakeholders, referred to as *public responsibility*, *corporate social responsibility*, *stakeholder relations*, or *external affairs* committees.

The Audit Committee

The audit committee is charged with assisting the board in its oversight of (a) the integrity of the company's financial statements and internal controls; (b) compliance with legal and regulatory requirements, as well as the company's ethical standards and policies; (c) the qualifications and independence of the company's independent auditor and the performance of the company's internal audit function and its independent auditors; and (d) preparing the audit committee report for inclusion in the company's annual proxy statement. The committee typically consists of no fewer than three members, all of whom must meet the independence and experience requirements of the NYSE and rule 10A-3 under the Securities Exchange Act of 1934, which hold that each member of the Committee must be financially "literate" and at least one member of the committee must have accounting or related financial management expertise (the so-called audit committee financial expert). Its members, including the committee chair, usually are appointed by the board on the recommendation of the nominating and governance committee.

The Nominating (and Governance) Committee

The nominating (and governance) committee has multifacetted responsibilities and is typically charged with recommending new candidates for the board of directors and determining (a) the eligibility of proposed candidates, (b) reviewing the company's governance principles and practices, (c) establishing and overseeing self-assessment by the board, (d) recommending director compensation, and (e) implementing succession planning for the CEO. The nominating (and governance) committee normally consists of three or more independent directors; its members and chair are usually appointed by the board on the recommendation of the chairman of the board.

The Compensation Committee

The compensation committee is charged with duties related to human resources policies and procedures, employee benefit plans, and compensation. It is also responsible for preparing a report on executive compensation for inclusion in the company's annual proxy statement. It typically consists of three or more independent members; its members are normally appointed by the board on the recommendation of the chairman of the board with the concurrence of the nominating (and governance) committee.

Other Board Committees

In addition to these standing committees, a growing number of companies make use of ad hoc committees to address specific issues—a *strategy* committee to look at different growth options, for example, or a *finance* committee to develop recommendations to recapitalize the company. While ad hoc committees can be useful, they should have clear sunset clauses to prevent their institutionalization or a balkanization of the board on important issues.

Committees can also be used to send specific signals to employees or external stakeholders about what is important to the company. A growing number of boards are creating committees to better communicate with and stay abreast of the concerns of external stakeholders. Names for such committees include the *corporate social responsibility, stakeholder relations, external affairs,* or *public responsibilities* committees. For example, the board of General Electric has created a public responsibilities committee to review and oversee the company's positions on corporate social responsibilities and public issues of significance that affect investors and other GE key stakeholders.

Finally, most bylaws make provision for an *executive committee,* usually consisting of the chair, the CEO and other designated officers of the company, and key directors, such as the chairs of the standing committees. In theory, the executive committee has the power to act for the full board in case of emergencies or when there is no time for the full board to meet and deliberate, although this is fraught with danger. Fortunately, advances in communication technology have made executive committees increasingly redundant, and their use has all but disappeared from the corporate governance landscape.

Director Compensation

Setting director pay typically is not done by the compensation committee of the board. Rather, director pay decisions normally are made by the nominating committee. The justification for this structure is twofold. First, it provides for a separation of the director and executive compensation decisions. Second, it allows the nominating committee to integrate compensation with board-building strategies.

The job of director has become significantly more challenging in recent years; it demands stronger qualifications, requires more time, and increasingly carries personal financial risk. In this new governance climate, the pool of available independent directors has shrunk and pushed up director pay. Directors are typically paid with a mix of cash and equity, with equity representing about half of the total direct compensation. Nonemployee chair and lead-director pay is generally structured like that of other directors on the board (retainer, meeting fees, and equity), while employee, non-CEO chairs are typically paid like an employee (salary, incentives, and benefits). A majority of companies pay a premium to committee chairs—especially audit and compensation committee chairs—reflecting the increased time commitment and additional responsibility. With respect to the equity component of director compensation, companies have reduced their reliance on stock options and increased the use of full-value awards.

CHAPTER 4

Recent U.S. Governance Reforms

Recent Governance Reforms: An Executive Summary[1]

In the aftermath of the governance scandals around the turn of the century, the government, regulatory authorities, stock exchanges, investors, ordinary citizens, and the press all began to scrutinize the behavior of corporate boards much more carefully than they had at anytime before. The result was an avalanche of structural and procedural reforms aimed at making boards more responsive, more proactive, and more accountable, and at restoring public confidence in U.S. business institutions.

The congress passed the Sarbanes-Oxley Act of 2002, which imposes significant new disclosure and corporate governance requirements for public companies and also provides for substantially increased liability under the federal securities laws for public companies and their executives and directors. Subsequently, the NYSE, NASDAQ, and AMEX adopted more comprehensive reporting requirements for listed companies, and the Securities and Exchange Commission (SEC) issued a host of new regulations aimed at strengthening transparency and accountability through more timely and accurate disclosure of information about corporate performance.

The most important changes concern director independence and the composition and responsibilities of the audit, nominating, and compensation committees. Additional reforms address shareholder approval of equity compensation plans, codes of ethics and conduct, the certification of financial statements by executives, payments to directors and officers of the corporation, the creation of an independent accounting oversight board, and the disclosure of internal controls. They are described in some detail in Appendix A of this book.

It is important to understand the rationale behind some of the most far-reaching reforms. The rationale for increasing *director independence* was that shareholders, by virtue of their inability to directly monitor management behavior, rely on the board of directors to perform critical monitoring activities and that the board's monitoring potential is reduced or perhaps eliminated when management itself effectively controls the actions of the board. Additionally, outside directors may lack independence through various affiliations with the company and may be inclined to support management's decisions in hopes of retaining their relationship with the firm. Requiring a board to have a majority of independent directors, therefore, increases the quality of board oversight and lessens the possibility of damaging conflicts of interest.

Audit committee reforms are among the most important changes mandated by Sarbanes-Oxley. The reasons behind these reforms are self-evident. Audit committees are in the best position within the company to identify and act in instances where top management may seek to misrepresent reported financial results. An audit committee composed entirely of outside independent directors can provide independent recommendations to the company's board of directors. The responsibilities of the audit committee include review of the internal audit department, review of the annual audit plan, review of the annual reports and the results of the audit, selection and appointment of external auditors, and review of the internal accounting controls and safeguard of corporate assets.

Compensation committee reforms respond to the unprecedented growth in compensation for top executives and a dramatic increase in the ratio between the compensation of executives and their employees over the last 2 decades. A reasonable and fair compensation system for executives and employees is fundamental to the creation of long-term corporate value. The responsibility of the compensation committee is to evaluate and recommend the compensation of the firm's top executive officers, including the CEO. To fulfill this responsibility objectively, it is necessary that the compensation committee be composed entirely of outside independent directors.

Nominating new board members is one of the board's most important functions. It is the responsibility of the *nominating committee* to nominate individuals to serve on the company's board of directors. Placing this responsibility in the hands of an independent nominating committee increases the likelihood that chosen individuals will be more willing to act as advocates for the shareholders and other stakeholders and be less beholden to management.

Analysis: Stronger Governance or Regulatory Overkill?

To assess the efficacy of the new regulations, it is useful to ask whether Sarbanes-Oxley, the new accounting rules, or any of the other reforms would have prevented some or all of the (U.S.) 2001 scandals. In an insightful paper, Edwards asks four key questions:[2]

1. What motivated executives to engage in fraud and earnings mismanagement? Or, put differently, is there a fundamental misalignment between management's and shareholder interests and, if so, what are the causes of this misalignment?[3]
2. Why did boards either condone or fail to recognize and stop managerial misconduct and allow managers to deceive shareholders and investors? Are the incentives of board members properly aligned with those of shareholders?
3. Why did external gatekeepers (e.g., auditors, credit rating agencies, and securities analysts) fail to uncover the financial fraud and earnings manipulation, and alert investors to potential discrepancies and problems? What are the incentives of gatekeepers, and are these consistent with those of shareholders and investors?
4. Why were shareholders themselves not more vigilant in protecting their interests, especially large institutional investors? What does this say about the motivations and incentives of money managers?

The Link Between Compensation Structure and Earnings (Mis)Management

As Edwards notes, it is now widely recognized that the dramatic changes in the compensation structure of American executives adopted in the

1990s were a significant contributing factor to the higher incidence of "earnings (mis)management." Consider that, in 1989, only less than 5% of the median CEO pay of the Standard & Poor's 500 industrial companies was equity-based—95% or more consisted of salary and cash bonuses—but by 2001, equity-based components had grown to two thirds of the median CEO compensation.[4] Since stock options accounted for most of this increase, executive pay became far more sensitive to short-term corporate swings in performance.[5] As long as stock prices climbed, executives could exercise these options profitably. The incentive to report (or misreport) continued favorable company performance was therefore substantial. Enron's executive compensation was closely linked to shareholder value. Enron senior managers, therefore, had a strong incentive to increase earnings and the company's (short-term) stock price.[6]

This analysis suggests that we must reevaluate how equity-based compensation is used to motivate executives and, in particular, whether there are pay structures that mitigate or eliminate incentives to misreport. The basic rationale behind equity-based compensation is sound: to motivate managers and better align manager and stockholder interests. But such pay structures must promote long-term value creation rather than reward short-term fluctuations in share prices.

Were Boards Asleep at the Switch?

Why were boards not more alert to managerial misbehavior? To answer this question, Edwards once again turns to the Enron scandal.[7] The company met or exceeded most governance standards. Its 14-member board had only 2 internal executives: its chairman and former CEO Kenneth Lay and President and CEO Jeffrey Skilling. The remainder of the board consisted of 5 CEOs, 4 academics, a professional investor, the former president of one of Enron's wholly owned subsidiaries, and a former U.K. politician. So, on paper, at least, the vast majority of Enron's directors met the "independence" requirement.[8] Moreover, all had a significant ownership stake in Enron, so their interests should have been aligned with those of Enron's shareholders.[9]

Enron's board structure was also strong; the audit (and compliance), compensation (and management development), and nominating (and corporate governance) committees all were made up outside independent directors. In fact, the audit committee's state-of-the-art charter made it the "overseer of Enron's financial reporting process and internal controls," with "direct access to financial, legal, and other staff and consultants of the company," and the power to retain other (outside) accountants, lawyers, or whichever consultants it deemed appropriate.[10]

Yet, what actually happened at Enron is very different. The Congressional Subcommittee on "The Role of the Board of Directors in Enron's Collapse" concluded that the board failed in its fiduciary duties (its duties of care, loyalty, and candor) because it permitted high-risk accounting, inappropriate conflict of interest transactions, extensive undisclosed off-the-books activities, inappropriate public disclosure, and excessive compensation.[11]

Whether or not this is a fair assessment of Enron's board performance, it shows that in an environment of short-term, equity-based incentives combined with less than transparent financial disclosure, the potential for manipulating financial results is real and that boards must be especially diligent. Many believe the Enron board did not meet this higher standard of care.

Would Sarbanes-Oxley and the new NYSE governance rules have prevented the Enron debacle? It is hard to say. The company already met some of the new requirements, such as independence for board members and key committees. Others, for example, the new rules requiring the elimination of conflicts of interest among board members and greater disclosure of off-balance sheet arrangements and other transactions to investors, might have made a difference. In the end, however, it is highly questionable whether ethical behavior can be legislated into being. Changing the ethics of business behavior and the "sociology" of the boardroom cannot be accomplished through structural changes alone; they require fundamental cultural change, which is a far greater challenge. In his 2003 letter to shareholders, Warren Buffett summed it up well when he confessed he had often been silent on management proposals contrary to shareholders interests while serving on 19 boards since the 1960s. Most boards, he said, had an atmosphere where "collegiality trumped independence."[12]

Did the Gatekeepers Fail?

What role could gatekeepers—external auditors, investment bankers, analysts, and credit rating agencies—have played in staving off the Enron and other scandals?

As noted in chapter 1, one view holds that gatekeepers are motivated and well positioned to monitor corporate behavior because their business success ultimately depends on their credibility and reputation with investors and creditors. Lacking this credibility, why would firms even employ gatekeepers? While this may be true, we should also inquire whether the interests of gatekeepers may be more closely aligned with those of corporate managers than with investors and shareholders. Gatekeepers, after all, are typically hired, paid, and fired by the very firms that they evaluate or rate, and not by creditors or investors.[13] This holds for auditors, credit rating agencies, lawyers, and, as we learned in a number of high-profile law suits, security analysts as well those whose compensation (until recently) was directly tied to the amount of related investments banking business their employers (the investment banks) did with the firms that they evaluated.[14] Thus, an alternative view is that most gatekeepers are inherently conflicted and cannot be expected to act in the interests of investors and shareholders. And while recent reforms separating consulting from auditing services, restoring the "Chinese Wall" between analysts and investment banks, and mandating term limits for auditors help mitigate these problems, it is unlikely that they would have prevented or minimized scandals, such as Enron and WorldCom.

Could Institutional Shareholders Have Made a Difference?

It is a basic tenet of free-market capitalism that the system rests on the effective ownership of private property—that is, that owners choose how their assets are used to their best advantage.[15] Yet, the largest single category of personal property—stocks and shares (including the beneficial interest in stocks and shares held collectively via investment institutions, mainly to provide retirement income)—lack effective ownership. Those who hold shares directly—in the United States, 50% of all shares are held directly—are individually so small as to be virtually powerless. Only if shareholders can unite effectively—and, in practice, this applies only to institutional shareholders—will corporate managements be held accountable. This seldom happens except in a rare corporate crisis, by which time the damage often has been done.

In the United States, more than half of all shares are owned by life insurance companies, mutual funds, and pension funds. So-called 401(k) plans, retirement savings plans funded by employee contributions and matching contributions from the employer, have become a major factor. Mutual funds compete heavily for this business. In theory, therefore, their corporate governance activities, if any, can make a crucial difference. With the exception of few public pension funds, however, institutional investors have not played an active role in monitoring corporations. Instead, they have been content to do nothing or simply sell the stock of companies where they disagree with management's strategy. One could argue this behavior is rational. Any other course of action is likely more costly and less rewarding for their shareholders and beneficiaries. Moreover, institutional fund managers themselves have serious conflicts of interests that incentivize them against direct intervention to prevent corporate misconduct. Their compensation—typically a flat percentage of assets under management—depends largely on the amount of assets under management. Retirement funds originating with corporations have been the most important source of new funds. Mutual fund managers, therefore, are unlikely to engage in corporate governance actions that antagonize corporate managers for fear of losing these pension funds. The law also discourages institutional investors from acquiring large positions in companies and taking a direct interest in corporate affairs, which would give institutional investors a greater incentive to engage in active corporate governance. For example, the "five and ten" rule in the Investment Company Act of 1940 is a clear attempt to limit mutual fund ownership, and section 16(b) of the Securities and Exchange Act of 1934 (the "short-swing profits" rule) discourages mutual funds from taking large equity positions and from placing a director on a portfolio company's board of directors.[16]

Thus, making institutional investors more active and more effective corporate monitors—while attractive from a theoretical perspective and consistent with the basic tenets of American capitalism—involves complex legal, structural, and philosophic issues: Should we encourage larger ownership in firms and more activism by institutional investors? What are the motives and incentives of fund managers, and are they likely to be consistent with those of shareholders? If we do want to encourage more institutional activism, do we want to encourage active ownership by all institutions and, in particular, by public pension funds, which may be conflicted by public or political interests? Finally, what structural and legal changes must be made to change the culture of institutional passiveness and bring about more activism?[17]

Synthesis:
What Is the State of U.S. Corporate Governance?

Has investor confidence been restored? Were the various regulatory changes effective? How sound is the American corporate governance today? As we begin to answer these questions, it is important to note that the U.S. corporate governance system has been roundly criticized and the subject of vigorous debate for many years. In 1932 Berle and Means warned that changes in ownership patterns would foreshadow "governance co-opted by management"; Mace has likened boards to "ornaments on a Christmas tree"; Drucker said boards "do not function"; while Gillies proclaimed that "boards have been largely irrelevant throughout most of the twentieth century."[18] A widely read book by Lorsch and MacIver has the colorful title *Pawns or Potentates*.[19] Perhaps the most cynical observation comes from an anonymous executive quoted by Leighton and Thain (1997): "Our board is like a bunch of ants . . . on top of a big log carried by a turbulent current swiftly down a river. The ants think they are steering the log."[20]

Robert Monks, pioneer among shareholder activists, founder of Institutional Shareholder Services (ISS), and well-known author on corporate governance–related subjects, recently expressed his skepticism this way:

There is almost universal agreement that corporate governance in America is failing. There was a large window of opportunity following public revulsion with the scandals of the 1990s. That energy has dissipated and virtually no "real" reform has occurred. We are in the "worst of times"—unignorable evidence of governance failure persists from the comic criminal of Health Care South to the nearly noble Royal Dutch Shell; equally unignorable is the failure on all sides to come up with credible improvement. Instead, companies complain of the cost of compliance with new laws and threaten to tie up proposals in appellate court litigation; reformers complain of the failure of new initiatives.[21]

Monks continues,

> Similarly, appearance and reality are conspicuously at variance with respect to recent governance "reforms." So much attention has been paid to such widely discussed "apparent" reforms as the NYSE listing requirements and Sarbanes Oxley ("SOX") that observers fail to note the fundamental difference between process and substance. Business leaders exacerbate the problem by polluting public dialogue with complaints of "governance fatigue." In reality, only a cynic or an incurable optimist could detect real reform in recent enactments.[22]

He concludes,

> I have recently argued that most of the observed problems of governance failure arise out of the excessive power lodged in the Chief Executive Officers. Persons having power are reluctant to give it up. This is the problem, and this is the challenge. Governance is stuck in the mode of confrontation between owners and managers and the managers have won. The informing energy of business is greed; solutions that are not based in economic incentives will certainly fail. Reform proposals will be credible only to the extent they make desired action profitable. Nothing by way of change will happen unless the various corporate constituencies can achieve profits through compliance.[23]

Real change, Monks (2005) argues, should focus on making shareholder responsibility a reality by removing the "many biases in the current legal/regulatory/institutional structure of governance." Monks makes a number of intriguing, sometimes politically controversial and challenging, proposals, such as placing a tax incentive on term owner-ship to encourage long-term holding of securities and discourage "churn-ing," increasing the role of shareholders in the nomination of directors to achieve true director independence, and splitting outstanding common equity into two classes—"ownership" and "trading" shares—to more meaningfully engage institutional owners in the governance process. Call-ing CEO compensation the "smoking gun" of governance failure, he also urges the restoration of CEO pay to credible levels, even if this means changing existing agreements.[24]

Despite all this skepticism, a reasonable argument can be made that the broad evidence is not consistent with a failed U.S. system. On the whole, the U.S. economy and stock market have performed well, both on an absolute basis and relative to other countries over the past 2 decades, even after the scandals broke. And while parts of the U.S. corporate gov-ernance system clearly failed under the exceptional strain of the 1990s, the overall system, which includes oversight by the public and the gov-ernment, reacted quickly to address the problems. On balance, most of the reforms that have been enacted are welcomed. Along with other increasingly common board features—periodic self-evaluation, for exam-ple, and requiring that directors own a significant amount of company stock—they have, by and large, had a positive effect on governance and, indirectly, on company performance. This is not to deny that significant issues persist, however.

Perhaps the most visible and contentious unsolved problem is run-away executive compensation. A growing number of investors and direc-tors, upset with absolute levels of pay and with forms of compensation that are not aligned with long-term corporate performance, want concrete change. Shareholder activists are pushing additional reforms. They con-tinue to press, for example, for the right of shareholders to directly nomi-nate and elect directors rather than work with the slate recommended by the board's nominating committee. Another proposal asks that share-holder resolutions receiving majority support become binding upon boards and that shareholder votes on merger proposals be made mandatory. Sup-port for these further proposals has been lukewarm, however, because they tend to undermine rather than strengthen the role of the board.

Others complain that the recent wave of reforms has been too narrow in focus—exclusively aimed at the immediate interests of shareholders—and has not addressed or even seriously contemplated the broader set of stakeholder concerns and societal pressures that is emerging on issues, such as companies' growing political influence, sustainable business practices, and various dimensions of corporate social responsibility.[25]

Finally, there is a growing concern that the recent wholesale adoption of new rules and processes may have had a number of unanticipated, unintended, negative consequences. Regulation is, and always will be, an extremely blunt instrument for solving complex problems, and impacts different companies in different ways. Many smaller companies, for example, are struggling to cope with the additional regulatory burden and comply with the new law. In recognition of this fact, proposals allowing smaller companies to scale back or postpone compliance with some of the provisions in the Sarbanes-Oxley are now under active consideration.

The Challenge: Striking a Balance

While no one disputes the need for transparency, honesty, and accuracy, corporate governance is about much more than the accuracy of the income statement and balance sheet. Compliance is a means to an end. The numbers merely summarize and reflect the full array of decisions—from strategy to structure to process—that guide a corporation. Encouraging responsible, responsive governance rather than mere compliance should be the overriding goal and the principal focus of reform. Truly effective boards understand their obligations to shareholders, other stakeholders, and society at large. They grasp the strategic challenges faced by their companies and the role they play in assisting management in seizing competitive opportunity. They also understand the dynamics of the interplay between management and directors, and they value partnership over adversarial relationships without sacrificing independence. And, especially in smaller companies, they alert management to opportunities for growth, assist in raising capital, and provide a sounding board for management on issues of strategy, asset redeployment, and fiscal and legal affairs.

Unfortunately, evidence is emerging that some boards have become even more "defensive" than before in the face of an increased exposure to shareholder and legal action. And, although there is no critical shortage of qualified directors at this time, it is not unreasonable to ask whether the new regulatory environment has made it harder to attract the right talent to serve on boards. It is, therefore, time to ask some penetrating questions: Has the regulatory pendulum swung too far? Do more regulated boards produce greater value? For shareholders? For other stakeholders? For society? Could the additional regulatory burdens reduce business productivity and creativity, or even board assertiveness, especially in smaller firms?

As we start to address these issues, we should realize that there is no unique model for developing a highly effective and responsive board, nor is there a unique model for what such a board looks like, how it organizes itself, or how it operates. It is also unlikely that it can be legislated and regulated into being. As noted earlier, changing the ethics of business behavior and the "sociology" of the boardroom cannot be accomplished through structural changes alone. Instilling ethical behavior and creating a value-creating orientation is fundamentally an internal process that can only be successfully concluded with the complete support of both management and directors. It requires openness to self-examination, a willingness to question individual and collective roles, a resolve to address issues of process, and a receptivity to change.

PART II
The Board's Responsibilities

CHAPTER 5

CEO Selection and Succession Planning

CEO Selection: A Key Board Responsibility

Selecting a new chief executive arguably is a board's most important responsibility. Yet, record CEO turnover points to distinct deficits in board performance in this area. The results of the 2007 Spencer Stuart Board Survey of the Standard & Poor's 500 companies provide important clues:

- CEO succession is on the board's discussion agenda annually at 62% of responding companies and more than once a year at 34%.
  - o Still, a quarter of the survey respondents said they do not have an emergency succession plan.
- Primary board responsibility for succession planning is split nearly evenly between the nominating and governance committee (41%) and the compensation committee (40%). The remaining survey respondents cited a variety of players, including the full board, all independent directors and management development consultants.
  - o Remarkably, when asked how the board involves the CEO in the succession-planning process, half of the respondents said that the current CEO leads the process, while a quarter said that he or she is involved at the same level as all other directors.
  - o Fifty-eight percent said that the CEO suggests internal candidates to the board or committee handling succession and contributes to their evaluation.

- Of the 53% of boards that use a formal review process to assess potential successors, 44% said the process includes benchmarking of internal candidates against external ones.
- Another study by Mercer Delta Consulting (2006) revealed that almost half of corporate directors surveyed were dissatisfied with their involvement in the succession-planning process.[1] Time pressures play an important role. Large majorities reported devoting many more hours to more immediate concerns, such as monitoring accounting, the Sarbanes-Oxley Act, risk, and financial performance. They also said they spent less time interacting with and preparing potential successors than on any other activity. This is unfortunate because the board's role in CEO succession is critical to effective governance; choose the right CEO, and all subsequent decisions become easier.

The list of high-profile failures is impressive: Gil Amelio of Apple, Durk Jager of Procter & Gamble, Doug Ivester of Coca-Cola, Jill Barad of Mattel, and, most recently, Robert Nardelli of Home Deport, just to name a few. All these former CEOs of major corporations have two things in common: They are talented, intelligent individuals with strong track records as managers and leaders, yet they all failed as CEOs. Some had been promoted from within to the CEO position, whereas others had been recruited from the outside following an extensive search. Some left on their own, whereas others were forced out.

The broader statistics are equally sobering; global CEO turnover set a new record in 2005, with more than one in seven of the world's largest companies making a change in leadership, according to Booz Allen Hamilton's most recent annual study of chief executive succession at the world's 2,500 largest public companies. Fewer than half of the outgoing CEOs left their office willingly, the vast majority left because of poor performance.[2]

What accounts for this high failure rate? Clearly, the job of being a CEO has become much more difficult in recent years, which, in part, accounts for their shorter tenures. In recognition of this fact, firms increasingly are splitting the function through a separate, nonexecutive chairman who deals with outside constituencies, such as customers, as

Intel's Andy Grove did, or with the financial community, as is the practice of U.K. firms. The model of the imperial CEO who commanded from the executive suite has long given way to the team leader model. In this model, CEOs are no less powerful, but the nature of power and influence has changed. Today's CEOs can only succeed if they enable others around them to succeed. Trust is the new leadership currency. In a world of instant communication, CEOs cannot be everywhere; therefore, they are compelled to rely on others as never before, and others will, in turn, rely only on those with similar core values.

One problem is that the vast majority of board members have little or no experience with CEO selection and succession planning. As a result, search committees often approach their task with only the broadest of requirements rather than with a well-thought out list of a company's real needs. The sociology of the selection process comes into play as well. As they screen candidates, directors may be seduced by reputation, when dealing with a Wall Street or media favorite, for example, or be blinded by charisma. However such inexperience manifests itself, the result is the same: Directors become so focused on what candidates are *like* that they fail to discover what candidates can and cannot *do*.

Succession Planning Is an Ongoing Process

Effective boards view succession planning as an ongoing activity that is integrated into the broader process of regularly thinking about the firm's evolving strategy and emerging competitive threats and identifying the skills top executives need to execute that strategy. They know which value-creating activities the firm has chosen as the cornerstone to developing a competitive advantage and what skills a CEO needs to implement them effectively. They are not caught off guard when a new chief executive must be selected because, as a matter of principle, they never stop thinking about CEO succession.

Reaching this level of performance is extremely difficult. Large companies perform literally hundreds of interrelated, value-creating activities, making it difficult for even the best boards to clearly understand how these many activities create value and what a CEO can do to affect the success with which they are carried out. To get there, boards must develop better means for systematically obtaining relevant, specific information about how the company creates value. In many firms, their principal source of information is a thick binder of market data and analysts' reports that is distributed 2 weeks before the next board meeting. How many directors have the time or inclination to comb through these binders? How do such masses of ill-digested information help them understand the value-creation process?[3]

An effective succession-planning process does not end with the selection of a new CEO. The board must be ready to coach the candidate it chooses, especially in the first months, and it has to agree on how it will evaluate the CEO going forward. Unfortunately, this rarely happens. More than half of the boards surveyed say they have little or no formal process for evaluating the performance of their CEOs, despite the huge responsibility entrusted to them. Worse, those who do often focus on short-term, easily measured business goals and give little attention to longer term objectives or metrics, such as the ability to lead people and manage stakeholders or professional ethics. This short-term bias is clearly evident when it comes to CEO compensation: Short-term factors continue to dominate the decision process and compensation formulas.[4]

CEO Turnover:
Different Scenarios, Different Challenges[5]

A top executive's departure has a significant impact on a company's operations, culture, morale, and ability to execute against objectives. This is particularly true when the departing executive is the CEO.

The reasons for a CEO's departure generally fall into one of four broad categories: (a) the CEO leaves to become the chief executive of another company; (b) the CEO retires or takes an extended leave of absence; (c) the board decides to replace the CEO with someone better suited for the current environment or for likely changes in strategy or market conditions; or (d) the company's board fires a failing CEO.

These first two scenarios force a board into a reactive posture; the departing executive initiates the event and the company must respond in some way. A board's ability to effectively respond to such a scenario depends on many factors, but its preparedness and the amount of time it has to react are perhaps the most important. Unless comprehensive succession plans have been in place for a while, boards may have little choice but to recruit an outsider. One of the most compelling reasons for an effective succession-planning process is that the board will have a better understanding of the skills and competencies needed to lead the company going forward, and therefore will be in a better position to decide whether to go with an insider or an outsider and what qualifications the ideal candidate should have. Thus, a well-thought-out succession-planning process enhances the board's ability to make an informed choice among prospects and broadens its portfolio of alternatives.

The last two scenarios involve a proactive change initiated by the board, and therefore represent different challenges. As painful and disruptive as it can be, the dismissal of a CEO often provides companies a much-needed opportunity to reexamine goals, strategies, and values. One scenario involves the replacement of an incumbent CEO who has been successful up to the present time but may not be the best person to lead the company in the future. Examples include the replacement of a company's founder whose decisions have become detrimentally biased by emotion, of a private-company's CEO by a professional manager with experience in taking companies public, of a growth company's CEO in need of a leader familiar with rapid multinational expansion; or of a CEO of a company facing unprecedented competitive demands. A second even more traumatic scenario involves the dismissal of an underperforming CEO or a firing for cause.

A board's decision to appoint transitional leadership during turnarounds, mergers, or acquisitions, initial public offerings (IPOs), restructurings, or other times of substantial change provides another example of a proactive change. The right interim CEO—tested in crisis and trusted by employees, creditors, and shareholders—can steer the company through its volatile period while the search for a permanent successor continues.

CEO Selection: Common Board Mistakes[6]

Many of the succession failures can be traced to a few common mistakes, all of which are exacerbated by a board's lack of preparedness.

The first occurs when emotion wins over reason. There have been several instances in which boards of high-profile public companies over-reacted when challenged with the appointment of a new CEO. One way this can occur is when a board, under strong media pressure and financial analyst scrutiny, feels it needs to act quickly and ends up choosing a well-known "star" rather than deliberately doing homework and carefully defining the specific traits, competencies, and experiences appropriate to the position.

A critical lack of knowledge of what works and, equally important, what does not, is a second factor. A board facing the departure of a CEO has a number of options, each with advantages and disadvantages. Unfortunately, three of the most popular CEO replacement recipes do not seem to work well in practice. The first is selecting a *prior* CEO, someone with experience as the head of another large public company. Prior CEOs appear to bring important advantages. Many of them have a track record of creating shareholder value and already know how to work effectively with a board of directors, communicate with investors and security analysts, and develop and implement strategy. There is compelling evidence, however, that prior CEOs perform no better and sometimes worse than new, previously untested CEOs. This suggests that prior CEO experience may not be as valuable as experience in the company, in the industry, or with the types of challenges the company faces. It also points to the need for candidates to have a high level of energy to take on a major new challenge.

The most popular CEO replacement strategy is *poaching* a currently successful CEO from another large corporation. This strategy also reflects the belief that executive leadership is a generic skill set, not specific to either the industry or company. The current evidence regarding the efficacy of this strategy is thin because only a few of these CEOs have completed their career. If, however, the generally subpar results associated with hiring prior CEOs hold true for active CEOs hired from other companies, poaching may also be a losing proposition.

Both the prior CEO and poaching strategies are based on the idea that bringing in an outsider is better than choosing someone from inside. While there are times when it makes sense to recruit an outsider, for example, when the organization needs to be shaken up, an outside search should not be the only option. Although some outsiders come into a company, rally the troops, and create a following, others are immediately overwhelmed by what they need to learn. Rather than being highly visible and engaged leaders, they lock themselves in their offices with a few key executives and volumes of data. And because they do not spend enough time with key customers, employees, and other significant stakeholders, they risk being viewed as outsiders. All other things being equal, inside candidates, at least, are familiar with the culture and the business, a trait that gives them a leg up on outside candidates. Unfortunately, when inside candidates are automatically ignored, outstanding executives and future leaders one or two layers down in the organization may leave the organization, imperiling succession down the road.

The third common replacement strategy—making the chief executive chairman of the board while promoting a second individual, from inside or outside, to the CEO position—is another example of a seemingly good idea that can be disastrous in practice. This *apprentice* model covers more than one third of all CEO departures in 2005. In theory, the apprentice model sounds great: not only is it consistent with best practice because it separates the roles of chairman and CEO, but it also keeps the skills and experience of the former CEO available and allows for mentoring the new CEO.

The practical evidence is more sobering. The 2005 Booz Allen Hamilton study compared three governance models: the combined chairman–CEO; distinct roles, with someone other than the previous CEO serving as chairman; and the chairmanship held by the former CEO. The results were unequivocal: the best performing companies were those in which the roles were split and the chairman was a true outsider, not the former CEO. The study attributes the apparent failure of the apprentice model to the inevitable ineffective division of responsibility and authority that it promotes. As the company's former CEO, the new chairman for many years set the direction for the company, controlled promotions and compensation, and defined the company's culture to both employees and external stakeholders. In his or her new position, he or she is likely to be approached by anyone who is unsettled by the successor's strategy or actions. In more extreme cases, if the former CEO is unhappy with either the direction of the company or its performance, he or she can get the apprentice fired and take back the CEO title.

There are other shortcomings to this model. Having the former CEO around to offer guidance creates the impression that the new CEO needs more training and is not yet really qualified to do the job, undermining his or her authority. And letting the former CEO manage the board—a board whose members know or appointed the former CEO or worse, were made board members themselves by that CEO—also hampers the new chief executive's ability to develop a good relationship with the board and gain support for his management agenda.

It should also be noted that the apprentice model is inconsistent with the new regulatory climate and the rise of shareholder activism. Sarbanes-Oxley stipulates that a majority of board members must be independent, reducing the number of insider slots, and that nominating committees consist entirely of outsiders. At the same time, shareholder activists strongly favor a model in which the chairman is an independent outsider.

A final common mistake in choosing a CEO is an over-reliance on executive recruiters. No executive recruiter can understand a company's challenges as well as the current CEO or the board. In the absence of an effective succession-planning process and a carefully articulated list of desirable qualifications, however, recruiters may be forced to substitute their own, more generic list of desirable CEO attributes. In the absence of specific directions, executive recruiters also tend to gravitate to the prior CEO and poaching strategies for the reasons described above.

Insider or Outsider?

When companies lack the culture or the processes to internally develop their next CEO, they have no choice but to look outside. More than a third of the Fortune 1,000 companies are run by external appointees. Recruiting from outside is almost always more risky than promoting from within because directors and top management cannot know outside candidates as well as they know their own people. Outsiders are often chosen because they can do *a* job, such as turn around the company or restructure the portfolio. *The* job, however, is to provide purposeful leadership to a complex organization over a sustained period of time. But, as noted earlier, the requirements for that larger job unfortunately are often not well defined by the board. What is more, a wrong outside appointment can have a devastating effect on a company's prospects. New leaders bring new talent and different management styles, thereby threatening continuity and momentum. In many such instances—as morale drops— the energy to execute dissipates as employees worry about the security of their job, and, rather than focus on the competition, companies begin to look inward. Bad external appointments are also expensive, since even poor performance is often rewarded with rich severance packages. That does not mean going outside is always wrong. Sometimes an external candidate exists who is, very simply, the best available choice. A skillful, diligent board may discover an outstanding fit between an outsider and the job at hand, as was the case when IBM attracted Lou Gerstner.

Just as going outside is sometimes the right choice, selecting an insider can be a big mistake. In fact, in certain situations, internal candidates present the greater risk. Some concerns about insiders, ironically, stem from their very closeness to the company. As Charan notes,

as "known quantities," they may sail through a lax due-diligence process. Or their social networks and psychological ties may complicate efforts to change the culture. Some will not have had the right experience or been tested in the right ways. Individuals from functional areas may not be up to the task of leading the entire business. Or a shift in the industry or market landscape may render carefully nurtured skills irrelevant. In some cases, the credibility of the outgoing CEO or management team may be so sullied that only a new broom can sweep the company clean.[7]

Grooming the Next CEO

Effective succession planning requires significant company investment and senior managers who understand and are committed to individual development. In today's ever-changing business environment, where lifetime employment is not necessarily desired and certainly not taken for granted, good succession planning helps high-potential talent acquire key leadership and managerial skills and is a useful way to retain important players.

Few companies are in the enviable position of General Electric or Microsoft, where positions at the director level and above usually have a minimum of two or three people ready to step in when the current jobholder moves on. Many companies do a decent job nurturing middle managers, but as the robust market for senior managers attests, meaningful leadership development stops well below the top. Even in companies with strong development programs, very few leaders will ever be qualified to run the company. General Electric had around 225,000 employees in 1993 when Jack Welch identified 20 potential successors; over 7 years, he narrowed this number to 3. As Charan notes, "In CEO succession, it takes a ton of ore to produce an ounce of gold."[8]

There are many challenges to developing the next CEO. To prepare candidates for a 10-year run in the top job, companies must identify candidates when they are around 30 years of age and expose them to the right challenges and mentors for a period of 15 or more years. Few companies have the skill, resources, or commitment to spot and evaluate potential talent this early and purposefully. What is more, most companies do not know how to provide their most talented managers with the kinds of experiences that prepare them for the CEO role. The development of the next generation of leaders requires creating challenging assignments and "stretch jobs" supported by coaching, mentoring, and action learning. Action learning brings high-potential individuals together to work on a pressing issue, such as whether to enter a new geography or launch a new product. It forces emerging leaders to look beyond their functional silos to solve strategic problems and, in the process, learn firsthand what it takes to be a general manager. Unfortunately, however, many companies still view succession planning as primarily a human resources function and equate leadership development with rotating candidates through multiple functions or cultural assignments. Although valuable, such an approach does not prepare a candidate for the unique challenges associated with being a CEO. Functional leaders learn to lead functions, not whole companies. Moreover, a major drawback of rotation-based development programs is that potential candidates often do not stay long enough in one position to live with the consequences of their decisions. The very best preparation for CEOs is progression through positions with responsibility for steadily larger and more complex profit and loss (P&L) centers.

A candidate might start by managing a single product, then a customer segment, then a country, then several product lines, then a business unit, and then a division. Whatever the progression, overall P&L responsibility at every level is critical.

Leadership development is only part of the solution. Boards can greatly improve the chances of finding a strong successor in other ways. Senior executive development should be an explicit element in the charter of the board's compensation committee. The committee should receive and create regular reports on the pool of potential CEOs and spend time getting to know the top contenders. Promising internal candidates should be invited to give presentations at board meetings and meet informally with directors whenever possible. Directors should also be encouraged to meet with and observe candidates in their own business operations. Finally, the full board should devote more time to succession; at minimum, the list of five top contenders, both internal and external, should be reviewed and updated twice a year.

The right process starts with the board's commitment to make succession a permanent agenda item for the board and to meaningfully link succession with strategic oversight. Directors must thoroughly understand how the CEO adds value, what the key strategy levers are that the chief executive has or must create to achieve the company's strategic objectives, and what skill sets and leadership attributes he or she needs to be successful. This requires that directors have a deep knowledge of the firm's competitive position and challenges, its unique competences, as well as its cultural and administrative heritage. Only this depth of knowledge allows a board to focus its search on the key executive skills and past experiences needed to effectively move the company forward.

As noted earlier, no firm can rely exclusively on developing new talent internally. Even in the most talent-rich organizations, fresh ideas and new perspectives are sometimes needed. Executive search firms can help bring in new talent from the outside but can only be effective if the board does its homework. Search firms can open doors; identify and screen candidates; conduct thorough, fact-based due diligence on candidates; and create a bridge between the board and candidates; however, they cannot tell the board what leadership qualities and experiences it should look for. It is incumbent on the board, therefore, to provide the search firm with a detailed profile of the skills, experiences, and character traits it thinks the next CEO needs to have.

In all of this, the role of the outgoing CEO, if he or she has one, should be mainly consultative. He or she must be active in spotting and grooming talent, help define the job's requirements, provide accurate information about both internal and external candidates, and facilitate discussions between candidates and directors. But they have no vote when it comes to choosing the successor: That decision belongs to the board.

Succession Planning: Best Practices

Succession planning is a dynamic process too often given short shrift when it is regarded as an human resources–led exercise rather than a high-priority, comprehensive board-led process. High-impact succession planning is a continuous leadership "optimization" process with the goal of identifying and developing a pool of talent armed with the skills, attributes, and experiences to fill key leadership positions, including that of CEO, as well as the cultivation of a talent pipeline to meet emerging leadership needs. Succession and development processes that are rooted in best practice principles have the following components:[9]

1. *Plan 5 to 10 years ahead.* A multiyear process is essential to develop and prepare internal candidates versus recruiting from outside the company.

2. *Involve the full board.* The full board is required in critical parts of the process (establishing criteria, evaluating candidates, and making the decision) and should not be relegated to a committee.

3. *Establish an open and ongoing dialogue and an annual review.* The board and the CEO should maintain an open and ongoing dialogue on succession planning. A review of the plan and candidate assessments must be held at least once a year.

4. *Develop and agree on a comprehensive set of selection criteria.* Criteria for the new CEO should be developed with the company's future strategic needs in mind and include bottom-line impact, operational impact, and leadership effectiveness dimensions.

5. *Use formal assessment.* Formal assessment processes from multiple sources provide information that helps boards objectively assess candidates and identify development needs.

6. *Interact with internal candidates.* Board members should be given ongoing opportunities to interact with internal candidates in various settings.

7. *Stage the succession but avoid horse races.* Candidates should be placed in a series of expanding roles that give them the opportunity to learn and grow, and allow directors to assess their abilities. The potential successors should never be publicly announced, so candidates do not feel they are competing for the role.

8. *Develop a good working relationship with an executive search firm to identify, screen, and attract external candidates.* While many boards prefer to develop internal candidates because they are familiar with the "territory," the pool should be enriched with talented outsiders.

9. *Have the outgoing CEO leave or stay on as chair for a limited time.* The outgoing CEO should either leave the board immediately or stay on as chairman for a transitional period of 6 to 12 months maximum in order to avoid potential leadership conflicts.

10. *Prepare a comprehensive emergency succession plan.* Emergency succession planning should be dealt with as soon as a new CEO takes the helm. The board should review the plan every year thereafter.

For some final wisdom on this subject, consider Warren Buffett's reassuring words to Berkshire Hathaway shareholders in his 2005 annual letter:

> As owners, you are naturally concerned about whether I will insist on continuing as CEO after I begin to fade and, if so, how the board will handle that problem. You also want to know what happens if I should die tonight.
>
> That second question is easy to answer. Most of our many businesses have strong market positions, significant momentum, and terrific managers. The special Berkshire culture is deeply ingrained throughout our subsidiaries, and these operations won't miss a beat when I die.

Moreover, we have three managers at Berkshire who are reasonably young and fully capable of being CEO. Any of the three would be much better at certain management aspects of my job than I. On the minus side, none has my crossover experience that allows me to be comfortable making decisions in either the business arena or in investments. That problem will be solved by having another person in the organization handle marketable securities. That's an interesting job at Berkshire, and the new CEO will have no problem in hiring a talented individual to do it. Indeed, that's what we have done at GEICO for 26 years, and our results have been terrific.

Berkshire's board has fully discussed each of the three CEO candidates and has unanimously agreed on the person who should succeed me if a replacement were needed today. The directors stay updated on this subject and could alter their view as circumstances change—new managerial stars may emerge and present ones will age. The important point is that the directors know now—and will always know in the future—exactly what they will do when the need arises.

The other question that must be addressed is whether the Board will be prepared to make a change if that need should arise not from my death but rather from my decay, particularly if this decay is accompanied by my delusional thinking that I am reaching new peaks of managerial brilliance. That problem would not be unique to me. Charlie and I have faced this situation from time to time at Berkshire's subsidiaries. Humans age at greatly varying rates—but sooner or later their talents and vigor decline. Some managers remain effective well into their 80s—Charlie is a wonder at 82—and others noticeably fade in their 60s. When their abilities ebb, so usually do their powers of self-assessment. Someone else often needs to blow the whistle.

When that time comes for me, our board will have to step up to the job. From a financial standpoint, its members are unusually motivated to do so. I know of no other board in the country in which the financial interests of directors are so completely aligned with those of shareholders. Few boards even come close.

On a personal level, however, it is extraordinarily difficult for most people to tell someone, particularly a friend, that he or she is no longer capable.

If I become a candidate for that message, however, our board will be doing me a favor by delivering it. *Every* share of Berkshire that I own is destined to go to philanthropies, and I want society to reap the maximum good from these gifts and bequests. It would be a tragedy if the philanthropic potential of my holdings was diminished because my associates shirked their responsibility to (tenderly, I hope) show me the door. But don't worry about this. We have an outstanding group of directors, and they will always do what's right for shareholders.

And while we are on the subject, I feel terrific.

CHAPTER 6

Oversight, Compliance, and Risk Management

The New Regulatory Climate

Complying with the new regulations has not only dramatically increased the workload and responsibilities of CFOs, finance teams, and directors, but it also has fundamentally changed their role and their relationship with other, nonfinancial groups within the corporation. For example, the provisions of the Sarbanes-Oxley Act call for senior finance executives and the audit committee of the board to take a much more active role in the operations of the business, as they are charged with certifying the strength of both a company's internal controls and the information they generate. Three sections of Sarbanes-Oxley are especially relevant: section 302, which outlines corporate responsibility for financial reports; section 404, which covers management assessment of internal controls; and section 409, which requires more rapid public disclosure of so-called material events in company performance.

Traditionally, the role of the *audit committee* has been to oversee, monitor, and advise company management and outside auditors in conducting audits and preparing financial statements, subject to the ultimate authority of the board of directors. The Securities and Exchange Commission (SEC) first recommended that publicly held companies establish audit committees in 1972. The stock exchanges quickly followed suit by either requiring or recommending that companies establish audit committees. In 2002, Sarbanes-Oxley increased audit committees' responsibilities and authority, and raised membership requirements and committee composition to include more independent directors. The SEC and the stock exchanges followed with additional new regulations and rules to strengthen audit committees.[1]

Fulfilling all of the duties and responsibilities assigned to them under recent legislation and newly adopted stock exchange rules and shifting to a more proactive oversight role represent major challenges for audit committees. Their responsibilities have been expanded in major ways and now include ensuring accountability on the part of management and internal and external auditors; making certain all groups involved in the financial reporting and internal controls process understand their roles; gaining input from the internal auditors, external auditors, and outside experts when needed; and safeguarding the overall objectivity of the financial reporting and internal controls process.

Importantly, in the wake of Sarbanes-Oxley, the relationship between management and outside auditors has been replaced by one between the audit committee and outside auditors. The audit committee now is directly responsible for appointment, compensation, retention, and oversight of independent auditors who report directly to the audit committee. And, by vesting responsibility and authority for certain audit-related actions in the audit committee—to the exclusion of the full board, management, and shareholders—Sarbanes-Oxley appears to alter the traditional delegation, under state law, of board power to a committee.

The audit committee must also establish specific procedures for handling complaints received by the company regarding accounting, internal accounting controls, or auditing matters, including confidential submission by company employees of concerns regarding questionable accounting or auditing matters. In addition, all audit services and permitted nonaudit services provided by outside accounting firms must be preapproved by the audit committee. All approvals of nonaudit services must also be disclosed in the company's periodic reports. Certain nonaudit services by firms that perform audits are expressly prohibited.

As noted in chapter 4, the composition and credentials of the audit committee are also tightly regulated. Public companies are required to have an audit committee consisting of at least three independent members of the board of directors. Each committee member must be "financially literate" and at least one member must be designated as the "financial expert," as defined by applicable legislation and regulation.

Audit committees are required to define their responsibilities and operations in an *audit committee charter*.[2,3] Such a charter should (a) clearly delineate audit committee processes, procedures, and responsibilities that have been sanctioned by the entire board; (b) define membership requirements, including a provision for a financial expert; (c) allow for yearly reviews and changes; (d) designate the minimum number of meetings to be conducted; (e) accommodate executive sessions with appropriate entities and allow for engaging outside counsel as needed; (f) outline the committee's responsibilities in regard to risk management, compliance issues, and review of its own effectiveness; identify the specific areas the audit committee should review as well as with whom those reviews will be conducted; and include such specific roles as annual report preparation oversight and yearly agenda planning; and (g) delineate the audit committee's relationships with the internal and external auditors; appoint, evaluate, set time limits for, and discharge (with the concurrence of the full board) the external auditors; and evaluate the independence of both the internal and external auditors.

Warren Buffett on the Challenge of the Audit Committee[4]

Often called the "Oracle of Omaha," Warren Buffett, the largest shareholder and CEO of Berkshire Hathaway, is well known for his adherence to the value investing philosophy, his conservatism when it comes to issues of governance and accounting, and for his personal frugality, despite his immense wealth. On the subject of a board's audit committee, he writes,

> Audit committees can't audit. Only a company's outside auditor can determine whether the earnings that a management purports to have made are suspect. Reforms that ignore this reality and that instead focus on the structure and charter of the audit committee will accomplish little.
>
> As we've discussed, far too many managers have fudged their company's numbers in recent years, using both accounting and operational techniques that are typically legal but that nevertheless materially mislead investors. Frequently, auditors knew about these deceptions. Too often, however, they remained silent. The

key job of the audit committee is simply to get the auditors to divulge what they know.

To do this job, the committee must make sure that the auditors worry more about misleading its members than about offending management. In recent years, auditors have not felt that way. They have instead generally viewed the CEO, rather than the shareholders or directors, as their client. That has been a natural result of day-to-day working relationships and also of the auditors' understanding that, no matter what the book says, the CEO and CFO pay their fees and determine whether they are retained for both auditing and other work. The rules that have been recently instituted won't materially change this reality. What *will* break this cozy relationship is audit committees unequivocally putting auditors on the spot, making them understand they will become liable for major monetary penalties if they don't come forth with what they know or suspect.

In my opinion, audit committees can accomplish this goal by asking four questions of auditors, the answers to which should be recorded and reported to shareholders. These questions are:

1. If the auditor were solely responsible for preparation of the company's financial statements, would they have in any way been prepared differently from the manner selected by management? This question should cover both material and nonmaterial differences. If the auditor would have done something differently, both management's argument and the auditor's response should be disclosed. The audit committee should then evaluate the facts.

2. If the auditor were an investor, would he have received—in plain English—the information essential to his understanding the company's financial performance during the reporting period?

3. Is the company following the same internal audit procedure that would be followed if the auditor himself were CEO? If not, what are the differences and why?

4. Is the auditor aware of any actions—either accounting or operational—that have had the purpose and effect of moving revenues or expenses from one reporting period to another?

If the audit committee asks these questions, its composition—the focus of most reforms—is of minor importance. In addition, the procedure will save time and expense. When auditors are put on the spot, they will do their duty. If they are not put on the spot . . . well, we have seen the results of that.

Legal Issues Regarding Oversight[5]

Much has been written about the board of directors' *Duty of Care* in the *decision-making* context, which requires directors to perform their duties in good faith and with the degree of care that an ordinary person would use under similar circumstances. Most directors are similarly aware of the protections afforded by the *Business Judgment Rule*—courts will not second guess directors' business decisions if the directors act on an informed basis and in good faith. By contrast, the *oversight* role of the board is less well defined from a legal perspective. The reason is that, in an oversight context, directors are not protected by the Business Judgment Rule if they fail to take action when they become aware of corporate impropriety. Many directors are unfamiliar with this less defined and stricter component of the Duty of Care.

In adjudicating claims, the law distinguishes between two scenarios: deciding there is no problem and ignoring a problem. When a board considers a situation and makes a decision that results in a loss, the Business Judgment Rule will protect a board's decision if the board acted in good faith and properly informed itself in the process. The protection of the Business Judgment Rule is not determined by the results of the decision but by the quality of the process employed. For example, when a board conducts a proper investigation and either takes action or consciously decides that action is not necessary, that decision, even if wrong, will be protected by the Business Judgment Rule.

By contrast, when a loss occurs because of a board's failure to consider a problem, there has been no process, there is no decision to protect, and the Business Judgment Rule does not apply. Instead, directors may face liability for breach of the *Duty of Oversight*. Rather than having a court defer to the directors' business judgment, the directors will likely be required to defend a negligence claim. Thus, when directors are aware, or should be aware, of material improper conduct, violations of law or other action that could result in material harm to the organization, the Duty of Oversight demands that directors investigate the matter and decide whether or not corrective action is needed. If the board fails to consider the situation, the board will be criticized for failure to supervise and may face liability under the Duty of Oversight. Specifically, boards can be held liable under the Duty of Oversight for failing to act when they know or *should know* of wrongdoing.[6]

Note that although the board may not take action in either case, the results in the two cases are dramatically different. The Duty of Oversight, therefore, creates an incentive for boards to respond to potential indications of wrongdoing in order to gain the benefit of the Business Judgment Rule.

How can a board protect itself? The law demands that directors investigate when there are red flags. If a director has actual knowledge of a material problem, he or she would be well advised not to wait for management to bring the topic before the board. Proper board action will always be the best defense to a Duty of Oversight claim.

Delaware law allows a corporation, in its certificate of incorporation, to eliminate or reduce the personal liability of directors for breaches of fiduciary duty, including the Duty of Care. Although the Duty of Oversight is considered a component of the Duty of Care, Delaware courts have not specifically held that such a charter provision would bar a Duty of Oversight claim.

Red Flags in Management Culture, Strategies, and Practices[7]

Analysis of corporations that have experienced major ethical and financial difficulties shows these companies have a great deal in common in terms of their corporate culture and management profiles, as well as their accounting and governance practices. On the basis of this knowledge, we can identify a number of early warning signals or red flags that boards can use to spot the emergence of a corporate environment and culture susceptible to conflicts of interest and management abuse. For a suggestive list, see Appendix B.

Individually, these factors may not be predictive of future problems. In groups, however, they define a heightened risk profile and should be cause for additional scrutiny and objective analysis. For example, the combination of aggressive management practices creating rapid short-term revenue and stock-price growth coupled with weak board oversight, allowing the CEO to rapidly accumulate personal wealth through stock-based incentive compensation, has been present in a significant percentage of recent problem situations. Risk of rapid financial deterioration in such cases is exacerbated when the company also operates with aggressive financial practices and high leverage.

Audit committees would be well advised to monitor these categories of higher risk characteristics based on their proven usefulness in identifying corporate environments that may be susceptible to rapid stock price and credit deterioration, as well as fraud.

10 Questions About Ethics and Compliance for the Board

Building a culture of ethics and compliance is an imperative for today's board directors. This requires senior management involvement, organization-wide commitment, an effective communications system, and an ongoing monitoring system. To ensure total commitment, directors must ask the right questions that will assist them in assessing whether an effective program is in place. The following set of questions is suggested as a starting point:

1. Does the tone at the top, as communicated by senior management, demonstrate to every employee that ethics and compliance are vital to continued business success? Does the organization's culture support making ethical and compliant choices?

2. How has the organization supported the ethics and compliance program through training and communication efforts?

3. Can you describe the process for assessing ethics and compliance risks within the organization? Has the organization ever performed a cultural assessment?

4. How is the current ethics and compliance program structured? Does it cover the organization's global operations? Has it addressed the

high-priority areas? Has the organization's ethics and compliance program and code of ethics or conduct been updated to comply with the requirements of Sarbanes-Oxley? Has the organization reevaluated its internal reporting mechanisms in light of Sarbanes-Oxley?

5. Does the organization have an ethics and compliance officer? Is a senior executive with adequate time, financial resources, and board access in charge of the program? Are there dedicated, full-time resources?

6. Does the ethics code include statements regarding responsibilities to employees, shareholders, suppliers, customers, and the community at large, and is it distributed to all relevant parties, including the board, employees, management, and vendors?

7. Does a reporting process exist to keep the board informed on ethics and compliance issues, as well as the actions taken to address those issues? Is ethics and compliance a regular board agenda item?

8. Is there an effective and utilized reporting mechanism in place to let all employees raise ethics and compliance issues without fear of retribution? Is there an anonymous reporting mechanism or helpline? Who fields the follow-ups on concerns raised through the helpline? Are audit committee members or the audit chair named as an additional outlet for employee concerns?

9. What type of ongoing monitoring and auditing processes are in place to assess the effectiveness of the program? Are the code of ethics and compliance program reviewed at least annually by senior management to determine if they need updating due to business, legal, or regulatory changes? Does the internal audit function conduct reviews? Are employee surveys conducted? Has the program been reviewed by outside consultants or experts for possible improvement?

10. Does the organization regularly and systematically scrutinize the sources of compliance failures and react appropriately? Does management take action on reports? Are employees appropriately and consistently disciplined?

5 Questions About Hedging, Derivatives, and Trading Risks

Increasingly, companies engage in hedging, derivative, and trading activities that involve substantial risks as part of their overall corporate strategy.

Although hedging activities, with derivatives or other tools, may mitigate or resolve risky positions, hedges are rarely perfect. In addition, because of the sophisticated nature of hedging, derivative, and trading activities, the risk exposure of a company is difficult to define, complicating oversight of such activities by a board of directors.

At minimum, the board of a company engaging in hedging, derivative, or trading activities should ask the following questions:

1. Where are the hedging, derivative, and trading risks embedded in the company, and who in the company is responsible for these activities?
2. Does the board of directors understand the nature and purposes of the risk positions being taken?
3. Are there risk limitations in place, and, if so, what are they and how effectively are they implemented?
4. What is the risk to reward ratio that fits into the company's strategic plan?
5. Does the board of directors have a glossary to translate the explanations that it is likely to receive?

Enterprise Risk Management: The Board's New Tool[8]

Whereas traditional risk management approaches focus on protecting a company's tangible assets and the related contractual rights and obligations, the scope of a new approach called Enterprise Risk Management (ERM) is much broader. ERM, discussed in greater detail in Appendix C, is more than crisis management or regulatory compliance. It is a tangible and structured approach to addressing organizational and financial risk. It is strategic in focus, aimed at enhancing and protecting a company's tangible and intangible assets on an enterprise-wide basis. Its basic premise is that uncertainty presents both risk and opportunity, with the potential to erode or enhance value. Value is maximized when management sets strategy and objectives to strike an optimal balance between growth and return goals and related risks, and efficiently and effectively deploys resources in pursuit of the entity's objectives.

Although the management of a company is ultimately responsible for a company's risk management, the board of directors must understand the risks facing the company and oversee the risk-management process. Best practice suggests that board committees should incorporate risk management into their charters. A company's governance and nominating committee, for example, can ensure that the company is prepared to deal with risks and crises by evaluating the individual capabilities of the directors, nominating directors with crisis-management experience, and considering the time each director and nominee has to devote to the company. The governance and nominating committee should also work with management to establish an orientation program for new directors and succession plans for key executive officers.

More commonly, however, corporate governance guidelines delegate the responsibility for risk management to the audit committee. Alternatively, a company may appoint a risk-management officer, form a risk-management committee, or assign responsibility to a finance or compliance committee of the board. The responsible committee or group should meet regularly with the company's internal auditor, the chief financial officer, the general counsel, and the head of compliance and individual business units to discuss specific risks and assess the effectiveness of the company's risk-management systems.

Codes of Ethics and Codes of Conduct

In 2003, to implement sections 406 and 407 of Sarbanes-Oxley, the SEC adopted a rule requiring a company to disclose whether it has adopted a code of ethics that applies to the company's principal executive officer, principal financial officer, principal accounting officer or controller, or persons performing similar functions. A company disclosing that it has not adopted such a code must disclose this fact and explain why it has not done so. Companies also are required to promptly disclose amendments to, and waivers from, the code of ethics relating to any of those officers.

A code of ethics (code of conduct, statement of business practice, or a set of business principles) is useful for establishing and articulating the corporate values, responsibilities, obligations, and ethical ambitions of an organization and the way it functions. It provides guidance to employees on how to handle situations that pose a dilemma between alternative, right courses of action or when faced with pressure to consider right and wrong.

A good code of ethics should be signed by the CEO and endorsed by the board of directors; it should focus on the values that are important to top management in the conduct of the business, such as integrity, responsibility, and reputation, and demonstrate a commitment to maintaining high standards both within the organization and in its dealings with others.

A good example is the code of ethics authored by Buffett for Berkshire Hathaway directors, executives, and employees, with his now famous advice:

> I want employees to ask themselves whether they are willing to have any contemplated act appear the next day on the front page of their local paper—to be read by their spouses, children and friends—with the reporting done by an informed and critical reporter.[9]

CHAPTER 7

The Board's Role in Strategy Development

Who Is Responsible for Strategy Development?

Boards are being urged to play a more active role in strategy formulation. If evaluating the quality of management's strategic and business plans, including the likelihood of realizing the intended results, is a key board responsibility, so the argument goes, should it not determine for itself whether the company has the capacity to implement and deliver? It is a good but tricky question. How might a board do this? What, for example, should a board do if management presents a bold plan for spinning off or acquiring strategic assets worldwide? Assume that the logic is consistent, that the plan makes sense, that the numbers look good, and that management has a convincing answer for every tough question asked by the board. Has the board met its fiduciary responsibility or should it seek an independent opinion to "audit" the strategic assumptions made by management and its consultants? After all, directors do not have the equivalent time and resources to review the details of strategies presented to them.

A strong argument can be made that if the board feels compelled to retain outside experts to review corporate strategy, it probably has lost confidence in the CEO and should simply fire him or her. Conversely, one can argue that hiring outside consultants is the most cost-effective way for the board to prove its independence and positively challenge top management. Which is it?

In attempts to provide guidance on this issue, numerous "codes of best practice" have been proposed in recent years urging boards to define their responsibilities with respect to strategy development as

- setting the ultimate direction for the corporation;
- reviewing, understanding, assessing, and approving specific strategic directions and initiatives;
- assessing and understanding the issues, forces, and risks that define and drive the company's long-term performance.[1]

As the simple example above demonstrates, however, reality is considerably more complex. Traditionally, boards have become involved in strategy mainly when there were specific reasons for them to do so. The most common are the retirement of an incumbent CEO, a major investment decision or acquisition proposal, a sudden decline in sales or profits, or an unsolicited takeover bid. In recent years, however, as regulatory and other pressures increased, many boards have sought to become more deeply involved and create an ongoing strategic role, for example, by participating in annual strategy retreats or through the CEO performance evaluation process. Still, in most companies even today boards limit their involvement to approving strategy proposals and to monitoring progress toward strategic goals; very few participate in shaping and developing the company's strategic direction.

There are a number of reasons for this. First, there is a longstanding concern on the part of both executives and directors regarding where to draw the line between having directors involved through contributing ideas about the company's strategic direction and having directors who try to manage the company.[2] Specifically, there is a widely shared belief that strategy formulation is fundamentally a management responsibility and that the role of the board should be confined to making sure that an appropriate strategic planning process is in place and the actual development—and approval—of strategy is left to the CEO. Even those who do favor greater director involvement in strategy say that the degree of involvement should depend on the specific circumstances at hand. A significant acquisition proposal or a new CEO, for example, may indicate the needs for greater board involvement.

Second, in the aftermath of the Enron and other governance scandals, many boards had to focus on internal issues and on digesting the new accounting compliance rules of the landmark Sarbanes-Oxley Act. In a number of companies, this turning inward has had the undesirable side effect that the board's decision making has become so focused on compliance issues that strategic considerations have taken a backseat.

Third, some CEOs simply do not want their boards involved in strategy discussions; they view the board's engagement in developing strategy as interference into their managerial responsibilities and a threat to their sense of personal power. Of course, the downside of this posture is that the board may not fully understand or buy into the organization's strategy and that board talent is underutilized. Taking this approach sometimes backfires on CEOs when formerly disengaged boards become overengaged and then make their CEOs "walk through fire" on tactics.

Fourth, there is the delicate question of how knowledgeable even the most capable directors are to assist with strategy development. Most are quite effective in dealing with short-term financial data. Strategy development, however, also demands a detailed understanding of more future- and long-term oriented issues, such as changing customer preferences, competitive trends, technological developments, and the firm's core competencies. A typical board of directors is poorly designed and ill-equipped for this task. According to a recent McKinsey survey, more than a quarter of directors have, at best, a limited understanding of the current strategy of their companies. Only 11% claim to have a complete understanding. More than half say that they have a limited or no clear sense of their companies' prospects 5 to 10 years down the road. Only 4% say that they fully understand their companies' long-term position. More than half indicate that they have little or no understanding of the 5 to 10 key initiatives that their companies need in order to secure the long-term future.[3]

Finally, while board meetings are conducive to questioning specific strategic assumptions and monitoring progress toward strategic goals, they are not a good forum for the more creative, elaborate, and nonlinear process of crafting strategy. Board discussions tend to focus on the implementation and tactics of an ongoing strategic direction. Revealing serious reservations about the underlying strategic assumptions sometimes not only is seen as distracting and inappropriate but also may be interpreted as a vote of no confidence in the current management.

The bottom line is that carving out a significant role for the board in strategy formulation is extremely difficult. First, as we have seen, there is the nature of the strategy development process itself. Characterizing a board's involvement in strategy on a continuum from "passive" to "active" is a dangerous oversimplification. A passive posture assumes that strategic decisions are both separate and sequential, that managers generate options that boards choose from, and that managers then implement the chosen option and boards evaluate the outcomes. An active conception assumes that boards and management formulate strategy in a partnership approach, that management then implements and both groups evaluate. In reality, strategic decisions often evolve through complex, nonlinear, and fragmented processes. What is more, a board can be actively involved in strategy without being involved in its formulation. For example, a board can "shape" strategy through a process of influence over management in which it guides strategic thinking but never actually participates in the development of the strategies themselves.[4]

Second, as noted, certain situations dictate a more influential strategy role for the board than others. For example, at times of crisis, such as a sudden decline in performance, a new CEO, or some other major organizational change, boards tend to become more actively involved in strategy. Other determinants of the degree of board engagement in strategy issues include firm size; the nature of the core business; directors' skills and experience; board size; occupational diversity; board tenure and board member age; board attention to strategic issues; and board processes, such as the use of strategy retreats, prior firm performance, and the relative power between the board and the chief executive officer, particularly in terms of board involvement in monitoring and evaluating this position. External factors include the concentration and level of engagement of the firm's ownership and the degree of environmental uncertainty.[5]

Third, as a consequence of recent governance reforms that focused on making boards more independent, many now lack directors with relevant industry expertise to participate effectively in shaping strategy—much less to reshape it in an increasingly fast-paced business climate. In the current post-scandal governance climate, even as the business landscape is becoming more complex, many boards continue to give priority to compliance-oriented appointments rather than visionary ones.[6]

Finally, there are the ever-present constraints on time and knowledge. To become meaningfully engaged in strategy formulation, boards must become much more efficient, particularly since their time has already been stretched in recent years: The average commitment of a director of a U.S.-listed company increased from 13 hours a month in 2001 to more than twice that today, according to Korn/Ferry.[7] Directors also need to become far more knowledgeable and proactive about grasping the company's current strategic position and challenges more clearly. To understand the long-term health of a company, directors must pay attention not only to its current financials but also to a broader range of indicators: market performance, network positioning, organizational performance, and operational performance. Similarly, a broader appreciation of risk—including credit, market, regulatory, organizational, and operational risk—is vital. Without this knowledge, directors will have only a partial understanding of a company. While boards receive and discuss all sorts of "strategic information," financial measures—probably the least valuable component of a board member's strategic information requirements—still dominate. Even with better information, time constraints may prevent a broader role for the board. Boards typically perform their strategic governance role in the course of a couple of hours at every third board meeting—annually supplemented by a 2-day strategy retreat. A more active role in strategy development requires much more time.

Despite these difficulties, Nadler (2004) argues that companies should try hard to create a meaningful role for their boards in the strategy development process. The key is to create a process in which directors participate in strategic thinking and strategic decision making but do not infringe on the CEO's and senior executive team's fundamental responsibilities. In such a process, the CEO and management should lead and develop strategic plans with directors' input, while the board approves the strategy and the metrics to assess progress. The direct benefits of such an engagement are many, including a *deeper understanding* by directors of the company and its strategic environment, a *sense of ownership* of the process and the resulting strategy, *better decisions* reflecting the broader array of perspectives, *greater collaboration* between the board and management on other initiatives and decisions, *increased board satisfaction*, and *more effective external advocacy.*[8]

But, as Nadler notes, while the benefits can be significant, broader board participation in strategy development also has costs. First, directors must have a thorough understanding of the company—its capital allocation, debt levels, risks, business unit strategies, and growth opportunities, among many issues—and that takes time and commitment. Importantly, they must engage management on the major challenges facing the company and have a firm grasp on the trade-offs that must be made. A second potential cost is that increased board participation can result in less management control over outcomes. Real participation means influence, and influence means the ability to change outcomes. A well-designed process yields the benefits of participation while limiting the amount of time and potential loss of control.[9]

A Framework for Board Strategy Engagement

To create a workable framework for board engagement, Nadler (2004) distinguishes between four, roughly sequential, types of strategic activity:

1. *Strategic thinking.* The collection, analysis, and discussion of information about the environment of the firm, the nature of competition, and business models.
2. *Strategic decision making.* Making a set of core directional decisions that define fundamental choices concerning the business portfolio and the dominant business model, which serve as the platform for the future allocation of limited resources and capabilities.
3. *Strategic planning.* Identifying priorities, setting objectives, and securing and allocating resources to execute the chosen directional decisions.
4. *Strategy execution.* Implementing and monitoring results and appropriate corrective action. This phase of strategy development can involve the allocation of funds, acquisitions, and divestitures.[10]

It will be apparent that the board's role can and should differ dramatically in these four development phases. Early in the process, the board's focus should be on providing advice and counsel about issues, such as the process followed, perspectives taken, the inside–outside balance of environmental and competitive analyses, and presentation formats. Later, when key directional choices must be made, the board's role becomes more evaluative and decision focused. Once directional decisions have been taken, reviewing and monitoring progress should become the board's primary focus.

Nadler organizes the various discussions and decisions the board needs to undertake into a multistep "strategic choice process":

1. *Agreeing on the company vision.* This step entails restating or confirming the company vision—a description of its aspirations in relation to multiple stakeholders, including investors, customers, suppliers, employees, legislative and regulatory institutions, and communities. Such a vision statement should be aspirational and paint a picture of what the company hopes to accomplish in tangible and measurable terms. Good vision statements talk about measures of growth, relative positions in markets or industries, or returns to shareholders. They provide a benchmark against which to assess strategic alternatives.

2. *Viewing the opportunity space.* This second step focuses on an analysis of the full array of strategic options the company should consider from different perspectives. For example, the analysis might look at different emerging markets, the range of available technologies to meet a customer need, the potential set of customers, or the constellation of competitors. Each of these presents a different set of "lenses" through which to look at the environment.

3. *Assessing the company's business design and internal capabilities.* This third step looks inward, focusing on an assessment of the company itself, including its current business design and organization. The objective is to analyze the relative strengths and weaknesses of the firm, including its human capital, technologies, financial situation, and work processes, among others.

4. *Determining the company's future strategic intent.* In this fourth step, the vision, the view of the opportunity space, and the assessment of the current business or organization are brought together to identify a future strategic intent. The purpose is to identify the most attractive opportunities for their vision and their capabilities.

5. *Developing a set of business design prototypes.* Having identified a strategic intent, the next step is to develop prototypes for each business design. It is useful to consider a number of distinct, viable options to provide the opportunity for real comparison, contrasting approaches,

and true choice. The final decision should be made against a set of criteria developed in the strategic intent stage. The leading choices should also be tested against current organizational capabilities to understand the nature of the challenges inherent in executing each strategy. When this choice is made, initial planning of execution is complete.

This process unfolds over a period of months, with numerous meetings, work sessions, and rounds of data collection and feedback, and provides a way of building board engagement. Perhaps more importantly, management will benefit from the board's informed point of view.[11]

The Board's Involvement in Strategy: Special Situations

Two dimensions of strategy formulation merit special attention because they require substantial board involvement and typically are subject to detailed scrutiny by investors and other stakeholders—crafting a capital structure for the corporation and dealing with a takeover, merger, or acquisition proposal.

Deciding on a Capital Structure

Deciding on an appropriate capital structure is a strategic board responsibility. Businesses adopt various capital structures to meet both internal needs for capital and external requirements for returns on shareholders investments. A company's capitalization shapes its balance sheet and is constructed from three sources of capital:

1. *Long-term debt.* Debt consisting mostly of bonds or similar obligations, including notes, capital lease obligations, and mortgage issues, with a repayment horizon of more than one year.
2. *Preferred stock.* Equity (ownership) interest in the corporation with claims ahead of the common stock and normally with no rights to share in the increased worth of a company if it grows.
3. *Common stockholders' equity.* The firm's principal ownership, made up of (a) the nominal par or stated value assigned to the shares of outstanding stock, (b) the capital surplus or the amount above par

value paid the company whenever it issues stock, and (c) the earned surplus (also called retained earnings), which consists of the portion of earnings a company retains after paying out dividends and similar distributions. Thus, common stock equity is the net worth after all the liabilities (including long-term debt), as well as any preferred stock, are deducted from the total assets shown on the balance sheet.

Debt Versus Equity

In deciding on a company's financial structure, management often seeks to minimize the cost of capital, whereas investors look for the greatest possible return. While these desires can conflict, they are not necessarily incompatible, especially with equity investors. This is because the cost of capital can be kept low and the opportunity for return on common stockholders' equity enhanced through what is called "leverage"—creating a high percentage of debt relative to common equity. Doing so, however, increases risk. This is the inescapable trade-off both management and investors must factor into their respective decisions.

The leverage provided by debt financing is further enhanced because the interest that corporations pay is a tax-deductible expense, whereas dividends to both preferred and common stockholders must be paid with after-tax dollars. Thus, it is argued, the lower net cost of bond interest helps accrue more value for the common.

Higher debt levels increase a firm's fixed costs that must be paid in good times and bad, and can severely limit a company's flexibility. Specifically, as leverage is increased, (a) the risk of bankruptcy grows; (b) access to the capital markets, especially during times of tight credit, may diminish; (c) management will need to spend more time on finances and raising additional capital at the expense of focusing on operations; and (d) the cost of any additional debt or preferred stock capital the company may have to raise increases.

Because of its tax advantages and stability relative to equity capital (common stock), some finance experts have argued that higher proportions of debt capital may be advantageous to corporations. Their advice is not always heeded, however. Although periodically companies use debt to buy back common shares, a practice that can improve stock performance, most large companies rely heavily on equity financing.

Companies tend to use debt under certain circumstances more than others. For example, the decision whether or not to use debt is often related to the nature and risks of the cash flows associated with the capital investment. When diversifying into new lines of business, companies that are moving into related fields tend to use equity capital and those entering unrelated fields tend to use debt. Ownership structure is another factor. Firms with a high degree of management ownership, for example, are less likely to carry high levels of debt, as are corporations with significant institutional ownership.

Changing Patterns

In earlier days, a debt-free structure was often considered a sign of strength, and companies that were able to finance their growth with an all-common capitalization prided themselves on their "clean" balance sheet.

The advent of *leveraged buyouts* (LBOs) of the 1980s brought a new twist to the capitalization issue. Because of their low degree of leverage, large corporations with conservative, low-debt capitalizations became vulnerable to capture. Corporate raiders with limited financial resources were successful in raising huge amounts of noninvestment grade ("junk") debt to finance the deals. The captured companies often would then be dismembered and stripped of cash holdings so the raiders could pay down their borrowings. In effect, the prey's own assets were used to pay for its capture. As a takeover defense, potential targets began to assume heavy debt themselves, often to finance an internal buyout by its own management.

By purposely leveraging their prey so highly (at times with current income insufficient to meet current interest requirements) that the company could not continue to conduct business as usual, raiders forced cuts in low-return growth avenues and the sale of those divisions, which are more valuable outside the firm. In the process, a significant amount of intrinsic firm value was distributed to stockholders—especially those who had bought in for just that purpose—at the expense of other stakeholders and the company's long-term needs. They justified their actions by stating that managers who operated with low leverage were either inept or feathering their own nest, or both.

Takeovers, Mergers, and Acquisitions[12]

Takeovers, mergers, and acquisitions are an integral part of corporate strategy and not only provide important external growth opportunities for companies but also involve considerable risks for the firm and its shareholders. A merger signifies that two companies have joined to form one company. An acquisition occurs when one firm buys another. To outsiders, the difference might seem small and related less to ownership control than to financing. However, the critical difference is often in management control. In acquisitions, the management team of the buyer tends to dominate decision making in the combined company.

The advantages of buying an existing player can be compelling. An acquisition can quickly position a firm in a new business or market. It also eliminates a potential competitor and therefore does not contribute to the development of excess capacity.

Acquisitions, however, are also generally expensive. Premiums of 30% or more than the current value of the stock are not uncommon. This means that, although sellers often pocket handsome profits, acquiring companies frequently lose shareholder value. The process by which merger and acquisition decisions are made contributes to this problem. In theory, acquisitions are part of a corporate growth strategy based on the explicit identification of the most suitable players in the most attractive industries as targets to be purchased. Acquisition strategies should also specify a comprehensive framework for the due diligence assessments of targets, plans for integrating acquired companies into the corporate portfolio, and a careful determination of "how much is too much" to pay.

In practice, the acquisition process is far more complex. Once the board has approved plans to expand into new businesses or markets, or once a potential target company has been identified, the time to act is typically short. The ensuing pressures to "do a deal" are intense. These pressures emanate from senior executives, directors, and investment bankers who stand to gain from *any* deals, shareholder groups, and competitors bidding against the firm. The environment can become frenzied. Valuations tend to rise as corporations become overconfident in their ability to add value to the target company and as expectations regarding synergies reach new heights. Due diligence is conducted more quickly than is desirable and tends to be confined to financial considerations.

Integration planning takes a backseat. Differences in corporate cultures are discounted. In this climate, even the best designed strategies can fail to produce a successful outcome, as many companies and their shareholders have learned.

Most studies carried out in this area show that the probability of a major acquisition or merger failing (as measured in terms of financial return) is greater than the probability of success. Empirically, the probability of failure increases with the size and complexity of the merger and with the degree of unfamiliarity with the target business. They also show that the buyer often pays too much for the target company because it is overoptimistic in terms of its ability to (a) do better than the existing management, (b) implement the synergies identified, and (c) integrate the target within its own company in a timely manner.

The application of new international accounting standards (and, more particularly, International Accounting Standard (IAS) 36 on impairment of assets) forces companies to examine the value of their assets, especially that of their intangible assets, on a recurring basis. As a result, each overpaid acquisition will inevitably result in impairment of goodwill, and, sooner or later, the board and management will have to publicly admit that their decision has destroyed shareholder value. This new regulation alone is a powerful reason for boards to go beyond merely approving major transactions and become much more actively involved in merger and acquisition (M&A) activity than in the past.

The very nature of the M&A process makes the board's involvement a particularly sensitive issue, however. An acquisition frequently results from a long, confidential negotiation process, often involving extremely technical issues, and its outcome is largely uncertain. These factors lead management to present the board with only summary and high-level information on the opportunity and to wait for the outcome of the process before organizing in-depth discussions with the board.

This is unfortunate because M&A activity represents a unique opportunity for a board to add value. Outside directors may have unique experience with the M&A process, particular intermediaries, or with all too often overlooked merger integration challenges. At the very least, the outside view offered by the board at an early stage may counterbalance the optimism of the executives driving the deal or the partiality of numerous experts pushing for its completion, resulting in a more "realistic" attitude to the opportunity.

Rérolle and Vermeire (2005) identify a number of useful best practices to assist boards in M&A planning and execution:

1. *Validate the strategic benefits of the transaction.* Every major acquisition must take place within an established strategic framework. Many mistakes are attributable to acquisitions that are justified only after the fact as a "strategic fit." At a minimum, the board should ask how the opportunity came about—whether it is something the company's management has been working on for some time, whether it concerns a business activity or market with which the company is familiar, and whether it represents geographical or other diversification.

   Also, rarely can an acquisition be justified solely on the grounds of the savings it will generate because they are often illusionary. It must either meet a need that has been clearly defined up front and which the company cannot meet using its own resources, or it must enhance the company's competitive position. In order to create value, the acquisition must make it possible to build a genuine competitive advantage or to decisively prolong an existing competitive advantage. The directors' role is to test the solidity of this premise.

2. *Verify that the price paid is reasonable.* Ultimately, analyzing an opportunity culminates in a valuation. Such a valuation should reflect a realistic assessment of (a) the intrinsic value of the target in accordance with a number of different scenarios, (b) the value of expected synergies (and the cost of implementing them), (c) the positive and negative impacts of the transaction on the value of the purchaser's company (e.g., management will have to devote considerable time to integrating the target, which may have an adverse impact on the purchaser's business activities), and (d) the price that management offers to pay and the terms and conditions of payment.

   Furthermore, when a proposed acquisition is of particular significance in light of the company's size and when there is a possibility of a conflict of interest or a challenge by the minority shareholders concerning the price paid, it is advisable to have a fairness opinion drawn up by an independent expert.[13]

3. *Ensure that a comprehensive due diligence process has been carried out.* Due diligence is of critical importance as it enables the purchaser to verify the integrity of the seller's financial statements, representations, and warranties, and to identify potential problems.

The due diligence must be based on broad (but relevant) objectives concerning the integration of the target. All too often, due diligence is mainly based on legal and accounting criteria, whereas the company needs to identify all the areas of major risk and, in particular, current and future operating risks, or others that may constitute an obstacle to effective integration. A comprehensive due diligence process covers items, such as an analysis of the target's competitive advantages and their durability, the identification of key people (in particular those that the company may rely on for the purposes of integration), and the measurement of the stability of the most significant customer relations and the long-term prospects of formal or informal alliances.

4. *Approve a specific integration plan.* Experience has shown that integrating the target is the most complex part of the M&A process. In spite of a broad consensus on this point, this difficulty remains largely underestimated. The board can play an important role in alleviating this major problem by asking management to provide it with an integration plan prior to concluding the transaction. In particular, this plan needs to include (a) a timetable for the integration program, (b) an identification of the main initiatives undertaken by management to recover a significant portion of the control premium paid, (c) an assessment of the human resources and expertise to be earmarked for the integration process, and (d) a detailed business plan showing all the costs and benefits associated with integration.

During mergers and acquisitions, boards tend to focus on the strategic, financial, and governance aspects of a transaction. They often neglect one of the greatest sources of value in many M&A transactions: the talent of the management team in the target company. Exercising due diligence about talent is as important as paying close attention to the balance sheet, cash flow, and expected synergies of a deal. By asking management a series of questions about human capital in a merger or acquisition, boards can contribute to a smoother transition to a single company, a better merging of cultures, the loss of fewer "A" players, and a stronger talent bench for the merged company—all of which should ultimately create more value from the deal.

5. *Organize the board's work so that it is able to assist management upstream.* The board's contribution will be even more useful if it is able to contribute to management's thought process as early as possible in the analytical and decision-making process. If M&A is a cornerstone of the company's strategy, creating a special committee may be a useful way to deal with issues of efficiency, confidentiality, and the constraints inherent in a long and uncertain negotiating process.[14]

Monitoring Strategy Implementation: Choosing Metrics[15]

A key determinant of greater board effectiveness in the area of strategy is the set of metrics the board selects to monitor a company's performance and health. The goal should be to identify a manageable number of metrics that strike a balance among different areas of the business and are directly linked to value creating activities. In addition to the standard financial metrics, key indicators should cover operations (the quality and consistency of key value-creating processes), organizational issues (the company's depth of talent and ability to motivate and retain employees), the state of the company's product markets and its position within them (including the quality of customer relationships), and the nature of relationships with external parties, such as suppliers, regulators, and nongovernmental organizations (NGOs).

In selecting an appropriate set of metrics, it is useful to distinguish between value creation in the short, medium, and long term. Short-term health metrics show how a company achieved its recent results and therefore indicate its likely performance over the next 1 to 3 years. A consumer products company, for example, must know whether it increased its profits by raising prices or by launching a new marketing campaign that increased its market share. An auto manufacturer must know whether it met its profit targets only by encouraging dealers to increase their inventories. A retailer might want to examine its revenue growth per store and in new stores or its revenue per square foot compared with that of competitors.

Another set of metrics should highlight a company's prospects for maintaining and improving its rate of growth and returns on capital over the next 1 to 5 years. (The time frame ought to be longer for industries, such as pharmaceuticals, that have long product cycles and must obviously focus on the number of profitable new products in the pipeline.) Other medium-term metrics should be monitored as well—for example, metrics comparing a company's product launches with those of competitors (perhaps the amount of time needed to reach peak sales). For an online retailer, customer satisfaction and brand strength might be the most important drivers of medium-term health.

For the longer term, boards should develop metrics assessing the company's ability to sustain earnings from current activities and to identify and exploit new areas where it can grow. They must monitor any threats—new technologies, new customer preferences, new ways of serving customers—to their current businesses. And to ensure that they have enough growth opportunities to create value when those businesses inevitably mature, they must monitor the number of new initiatives under way (as well as estimate the size of the relevant product markets) and develop metrics that track the initiatives' progress.

Ultimately, it is people who make strategies work, so a good set of metrics should also show how well a business retains key employees and the true depth of its management talent. Again, what is important varies by industry. Pharmaceutical companies, for example, need scientific innovators but relatively few managers. Companies expanding overseas need people who can work in new countries and negotiate with governments.

Creating a Strategy-Focused Board[16]

Fostering a strategic mind-set on the board is difficult and takes time. It requires rethinking its composition, how it approaches its responsibilities, and the way it interacts with management to help develop a strategic vision, although that must originate with the CEO. Progressive CEOs, for their part, must be able to articulate a clear strategy and have the personal confidence to build board teams that include experts who may be far more skilled in certain industry and operational areas than the CEOs themselves are.[17]

Rather than immediately seeking a deeper involvement in the strategy development process, it may be useful to ask boards to first seek a more effective balance between short- and long-term considerations in their oversight. As part of first step, they should identify and agree on a core set of metrics reflecting a balance that is tailored to the specifics of a company's industry, maturity, culture, and current situation. In turn, management should be asked to draw up a set of long-term strategy options that the board can test and challenge. Management then can develop a detailed plan for the board's final approval.

Ideally, this process unfolds over several board meetings and allows board members to probe specific strategic issues—does the company really have the ability to execute in a particular area, for example, and has it analyzed different options to enter the markets it wants to compete in? Finally, the board can play an important role in monitoring the progress of the plan and any changes in risk it involves. While the board can be selective in its focus on details, management must deal with all aspects of the strategic plan. Once accepted, the strategy can be expected to evolve over time, and therefore will require an ongoing dialogue between the board and management.

CHAPTER 8

CEO Performance Evaluation and Executive Compensation

CEO Performance Evaluation[1]

Regular, purposeful, CEO performance evaluation by the board is a cornerstone of effective governance. According to Spencer Stuart's 2007 Board Index, 91% of directors surveyed said their CEO's performance is evaluated annually; the remaining 9% conduct more frequent evaluations. Respondents also noted differences in implementation: 45% of respondents cited the compensation committee as taking the lead; the entire board oversees the process in 20% of the participating companies; the nominating and governance committee oversees in 16% of the companies, and the lead director in 12%.[2]

Performance evaluation at the CEO level is difficult. Rivero and Nadler (2003) note that the difference between a good evaluation process in which everyone wants to participate and one that becomes mere window dressing is the CEO's attitude toward the process and reactions to the feedback. At the same time, an ad hoc process sprung on the CEO can send the wrong signals about the nature of the board and CEO relationship. Both the CEO and the board need to make an investment to ensure that the process is well planned and part of the normal course of business. Minimizing potential problems at the outset, therefore, raises the odds of creating a successful, sustainable process. Common pitfalls to look for include the following:

- *Uncertainty concerning roles and responsibilities.* Confusion over roles and responsibilities is not uncommon. A clear charter helps, as do descriptions of roles and accountabilities, and time-lines and milestones. The director leading the process (typi-cally the chair of the compensation committee) should actively work with other board members to clarify expectations for their participation.

- *Lack of time and energy.* Time is the enemy of many board pro-cesses, and an elaborate CEO evaluation process that requires significant input from the board may be met with resistance. Yet, a well-designed evaluation brings structure and efficiency to many of the board's other responsibilities, such as oversight and setting executive compensation, thereby actually saving directors time in the long run.

- *Disagreement over criteria for assessment.* Considerable debate over the appropriate criteria for assessing performance is normal and healthy. Before moving forward, however, the CEO and the board must agree on the dimensions of performance and objectives. Disagreements should be resolved by appealing to the strategy and business needs of the organization.

- *Lack of direct information about nonquantitative performance.* Financial and key operational metrics are usually readily avail-able, but measures of softer dimensions, such as leadership effec-tiveness, often have to be designed specifically for the purpose of the evaluation.[3]

A well-thought-out process analyzes both past performance and sets goals for the future, and therefore assists the compensation committee of the board in making decisions about the CEO's future compensation and employment. A good process helps the CEO and the board to establish focus on the company's future direction by specifying a set of strategic objectives. This goal-setting aspect of the evaluation can also serve as part of the CEO's ongoing leadership development, with the board providing feedback about areas where the CEO needs to do a better job, learn new skills, or focus additional attention.

An effective CEO evaluation process, therefore, looks backward, focusing on accountability and rewards for past performance, as well as forward, focusing on future objectives and whether the CEO has the vision, strategy, and personal capabilities to achieve those objectives. Although these are distinct objectives, in practice they are often integrated into the same process. Time constraints often force the board to evaluate the CEO's performance over the previous year while simultaneously making compensation decisions, setting next year's targets, and discussing specific areas for improvement, often in a single meeting. As Rivero and Nadler observe, this is unfortunate because when the two objectives are not clearly separated, there is a clear danger that neither gets served very well.[4]

When time is short the developmental part of the evaluation is often skipped altogether, forcing the board to use the compensation review to set the CEO's future objectives. This approach is likely to emphasize *what* the CEO is expected to achieve (usually framed in terms of short-term financial targets) over *how* the CEO is expected to behave (such as giving more attention to developing future leaders). When this happens, the CEO is unlikely to receive candid, detailed feedback about his or her behavior and personal impact.

Dimensions

Defining an effective set of dimensions to be evaluated represents a major challenge. Based on the distinction made above between a CEO's impact on corporate performance and his or her actions and effectiveness as a leader, Rivero and Nadler identify three generic sets of measurements of CEO performance: bottom-line impact, operational impact, and leadership effectiveness.

1. *Bottom-line impact.* Most CEO evaluation and "pay-for-performance" plans are based on the assumption that the top executive has a direct and significant impact on corporate performance, and therefore hold CEOs accountable for the company's overall financial health. While important, relying solely on shareholder-oriented, accounting-based bottom-line measures as indicators of CEO performance has

severe deficiencies. Most CEOs know that their ability to affect the company's bottom line is indirect and often limited.

2. *Operational impact.* Operational impact refers to the CEO's influence on the company's effectiveness in operational areas, such as customer satisfaction, new product introduction, or productivity enhancement, and how well the firm implements its strategy. Operational impact measures often give a better indication of a company's underlying potential to create value because they are directly related to the immediate stock price, which is subject to market-wide volatility. While still subject to external and internal forces outside of the CEO's immediate control, this type of performance is more closely related to the CEO's actions.

3. *Leadership effectiveness.* Leadership effectiveness addresses how well the CEO carries out his or her responsibilities, both in terms of executing specific role responsibilities—identifying a successor, meeting with key customers and investors, developing a long-term strategy—and the quality of those actions—communicating with external stakeholders, energizing the organization, and gaining the confidence of investors.[5]

The three categories described above are generic. While the specific dimensions and objectives that are used vary for each company, there are some general principles that leading companies follow in selecting CEO performance objectives. First, their evaluations reach *beyond bottom-line performance*. Financial measures of corporate performance, while critical, capture only one aspect of CEO performance. To compensate for some of the limitations of bottom-line measures, it is important to include objectives that reveal how the CEO behaves as a leader, as well as the CEO's impact on the effectiveness of the organization. Second, they *focus on a manageable number of objectives*. One risk in attempting to capture multiple aspects of CEO performance is that the list of performance dimensions may grow too large to be workable. Too few dimensions, on the other hand, cause the process to be dominated by short-term financial objectives. Best practice is to use between 5 and 10 dimensions. Third, they *use separate objectives for chairman and CEO performance, even if it involves the same person*. In most North American companies, the CEO also serves as chairman of the board. It is important to evaluate performance in both roles. The chairman role can be assessed either as one component of a formal board evaluation process, or the dimensions of chairman effectiveness can be added to the CEO's evaluation process. Fourth, they *define measures for each objective*. Creating explicit measures to track performance against the particular objective is relatively simple for all bottom-line and most operational impact objectives. For "softer" dimensions this is more of a challenge but can be achieved. For example, leadership behaviors can be measured through rating methods that ask board members to indicate how often the CEO demonstrates desired behaviors and what impact these have. Finally, they *specify performance levels for each rating measure*. Explicit measures for each objective assist in setting performance expectations with the CEO. Specificity helps create shared understanding of the performance standards between the CEO and the board.

Best practice also suggests that an effective CEO performance evaluation process is integrated with the company's calendar of business planning and compensation review: Step 1 is focused on *defining the CEO's objectives*. Before the start of the fiscal year, the CEO should work with the compensation committee of the board to establish key business objectives for the coming year. Using the strategic plan as a starting point, this dialogue should produce an initial set of personal performance targets and associated measurements. After reviewing and amending them if needed, the final set should be discussed and approved by the full board. These targets can then be used to create an integrated goal-setting process that aligns the objectives of each leadership level in the company.

Step 2 is a *mid-year review*. Six months into the year, the compensation committee and the CEO should review the targets and progress against them. Such a mid-year review can provide great value for two reasons. First, it helps the board see how the CEO is meeting or exceeding targets and to identify areas that require closer attention. Second, it provides an opportunity to amend the targets in light of changed circumstances, such as rapidly changing business conditions.

Step 3 is the *year-end assessment*. At the end of the fiscal year, the CEO's performance should be measured against the previously established objectives. As part of this step, the CEO should be invited to provide a self-evaluation and be given an opportunity to address areas where targets were not met. The self-assessment is shared with the compensation committee and then the full board for input on the CEO's performance. Evaluations by all board members go to the compensation committee, which uses the results to determine the portion of the CEO's pay that is linked to performance. Before providing feedback to the CEO, the evaluation should first be discussed by the board in executive session, that is—without the CEO or other inside directors present.[6]

Executive Compensation

A reasonable and fair compensation system for executives and employees is fundamental to the creation of long-term corporate value. However, the past 2 decades have seen an unprecedented growth in compensation for top executives and a dramatic increase in the ratio between the compensation of executives and their employees. "Runaway" executive compensation has become the subject of editorials, political debates, and battles between directors and shareholders. The reasons are not hard to understand; the numbers involved are large.

How Much Is Too Much?

In 2007, the CEO of a Standard & Poor's 500 company received, on average, $14.2 million in total compensation, according to the Corporate Library, a corporate governance research firm. The median compensation package received was $8.8 million, more than 350 times the pay of the average U.S. worker.[7]

According to the Economic Research Institute (ERI), executive compensation has grown substantially faster than corporate earnings in recent years. The study of 45 randomly selected public companies found that executive compensation increased 20.5% in 2007, while revenues grew just 2.8%.[8] Moreover, while performance-based bonuses for chief executives of large public companies dropped in 2007, companies more than made up for that decline by giving out bigger discretionary bonuses and other payments not tied to a specific financial target, according to Equilar, the executive compensation research firm.[9] Equilar found that the median value of bonuses tied to performance fell 18.6% in 2007, from $949,249 to $772,717. Thanks, however, to sizable increases in discretionary awards and multiyear performance awards, overall CEO bonuses for 2007 increased 1.4 % to a median value of $1.41 million from $1.39 million in 2006.

Excessive CEO pay takes dollars out of the pockets of shareholders—including the retirement savings of America's working families. Moreover, a poorly designed executive compensation package can reward decisions that are not in the long-term interests of a company, its shareholders, and employees.

Some CEOs may have far greater control over their pay than anybody previously suspected. Angelo Mozilo, chairman and CEO of Countrywide Financial Corp., brought in a second compensation consultant to renegotiate his package in 2006 when the first consultant said his pay package was inflated.

In an e-mail message to John England of Towers Perrin, the executive compensation consultancy who helped redo his pay package, Mozilo complained, "Boards have been placed under enormous pressure by the left-wing anti-business press and the envious leaders of unions and other so-called 'CEO Comp Watchers.'"[10]

While simply comparing a CEO's compensation to that of an average worker is not appropriate because it does not consider value creation, it makes for good press. So do high-profile reports of CEOs receiving compensation packages worth millions of dollars while shareholders lost a major part, if not all, of their investment and workers suffered benefit or job cuts. Such headlines fan the perception that despite new NASDAQ and NYSE rules mandating greater board autonomy, many directors remain beholden to management when it comes to compensation.

The CEO pay debate achieved international prominence in the early 1990s. An important milestone was the publication of Graef Crystal's exposé on CEO pay, *In Search of Excess*, which clearly demonstrated the prevalence of excessive executive compensation practices in U.S. companies.[11] *Time* magazine labeled CEO pay as the "populist issue that no politician can resist," and CEO pay became a major political issue in the United States.[12] Legislation was introduced in the House of Representatives disallowing deductions for compensation exceeding 25 times the lowest paid worker, and the Corporate Pay Responsibility Act was introduced in the Senate to give shareholders more rights to propose compensation-related policies. The Securities and Exchange Commission (SEC) preempted the pending Senate bill in February 1992 by requiring companies to include nonbinding shareholder resolutions about CEO pay in company proxy statements, and announced sweeping new rules affecting the disclosure of top-executive compensation in the annual proxy statement in October 1992.[13] In 1994, the Bill Clinton tax act (the Omnibus Budget Reconciliation Act of 1993) defined nonperformance-related compensation in excess of $1 million as "unreasonable" and therefore not deductible as an ordinary business expense for corporate income tax purposes.

Ironically, although the objective was to reduce "excessive" CEO pay, the ultimate outcome was a significant increase in executive compensation, driven by an escalation in option grants that satisfied the new IRS regulations and allowed pay significantly in excess of $1 million to be tax deductible to the corporation. Once the act defined $1 million compensation as reasonable, many companies increased cash compensation to $1 million and then began to add on performance-based pay components that satisfied the act.[14]

Stock Options

A principal driver behind the dramatic increases in executive pay in large U.S. firms over the past 3 decades has been the explosion in grants of stock options. A stock option is a right to buy shares at a particular price—the so-called strike price—at some future date. If an employee receives an option to buy 100 shares at a $5 strike price and the stock has risen to $10 by the vesting period, the employee can buy at the lower price and reap a quick profit. The idea is to align employees' interests with those of shareholders' to encourage productivity and profits. In reality the excessive use of options created a mechanism for companies to transfer profits directly to employees—mostly top executives—at the expense of shareholders.

The significant increase in the use and value of stock option awards was driven by a greater focus on equity-based compensation and changes in disclosure and tax rules that reinforced stronger linkages between stock performance and executive pay. Regrettably, there also is evidence that many boards and executives viewed options as a low-cost or even cost-free way to compensate executives.

In economic terms, the cost to the corporation of granting an option to an employee is the opportunity cost the firm gives up by not selling the option in the market, and that cost should be recognized in the firm's accounting statements as an expense. When a company grants an option to an employee, it bears an economic cost equal to what an outside investor would pay for the option. However, because employees are more risk averse and undiversified than shareholders, and because they are prohibited from trading the options or taking actions to hedge their risk (such as short-selling company stock), employees will naturally value options less than they cost the company to grant.[15] Thus, because the company's cost can exceed the perceived value to the employee, rather than being a low-cost way of compensating employees options constitute an expensive compensation mechanism. Its use can therefore only be justified when the productivity benefits the company expects to get from awarding costly options exceed the pay premium that must be offered to employees receiving the options.

Until recently, many U.S. companies were not very diligent in assessing the cost and value of options and treated options as being cost-free. Option grants do not incur a cash outlay and, until the recent change in accounting rules, did not bear an accounting charge. Moreover, when an option is exercised, the company incurs no cash outlay and receives a cash benefit in the form of a tax deduction for the spread between the stock price and the exercise price. These factors make the "perceived cost" of an option to the company much lower than the economic cost, and often even lower than the value of the option to the employee. As a result, many options were granted to many people, and options with favorable accounting treatment were preferred over better incentive plans with less favorable accounting treatment.

The impact of the excessive use of stock options, especially by leading technology companies, however well intended (ostensibly to attract, reward, and retain executive talent), goes well beyond the realm of executive compensation; it transferred a significant amount of wealth from share-holders to employees.

More recently the image of stock options was tainted further by two illegal acts—backdating and spring loading. Backdating involves picking a date when the stock was trading at an even lower price than the date of the options grant, resulting in an instant profit. Spring loading involves the granting of options right before a company announces news guaranteed to drive up the share price.

Backdating and spring loading violate existing accounting rules, state corporate law, federal securities laws, and tax laws. In a few instances, the U.S. Department of Justice has concluded that CEOs who backdated options committed criminal fraud. The recent backdating scandals forced numerous CEOs and other corporate officials to resign or be fired, and the SEC continues to investigate possible options backdating at more than 100 companies.

Backdating and spring loading also harm shareholders. The money paid to CEOs who improperly backdate or spring load their stock options belongs to shareholders, and when companies have to restate their earn-ings and pay additional taxes, shareholders lose even more. Since the Sarbanes-Oxley Act became law in 2002, companies must report stock options grants to their executives within 2 business days. Thanks to this investor protection law, it is much harder for executives to backdate stock options. But, Sarbanes-Oxley not withstanding, CEOs can still inappro-priately time stock option exercises based on inside information or by spring loading their stock option grants.

In the last few years, investors submitted dozens of shareholder pro-posals seeking to limit executive severance and realign pay with perfor-mance. Although boards have tended to resist such proposals, contending they constrain their ability to attract, retain, and motivate managers, they have started to change their pay practices to better align interests with shareholders. PepsiCo, for example, replaced its traditional stock options with performance-based restricted shares that are worthless unless earn-ings targets are met. And at Merrill Lynch, all but 2% of the CEO's pay package now consists of restricted shares untouchable until 2009. In 2003, almost 50% of the CEO's pay package consisted of cash.

Golden Parachutes

A "golden parachute," or change-of-control agreement, is an agreement that provides key executives with generous severance pay and other benefits in the event that their employment is terminated as a result of a change of ownership of the company. Golden parachutes are voted on by the board and, depending on the laws of the state in which the company is incorporated, may require shareholder approval. Some golden parachutes are triggered even if the control of the corporation does not change completely; such parachutes open after a certain percentage of the corporation's stock is acquired.

Golden parachutes have been justified on three grounds. First, they may enable corporations that are prime takeover targets to hire and retain high-quality executives who would otherwise be reluctant to work for them. Second, since the parachutes add to the cost of acquiring a corporation, they may discourage takeover bids. Finally, if a takeover bid does occur, executives with a golden parachute are more likely to respond in a manner that will benefit the shareholders. Without a golden parachute, executives might resist a takeover that would be in the interests of the shareholders to save their own job.

As golden parachutes have grown more prevalent and lucrative, they have increasingly come under criticism from shareholders. Their concern is understandable since many golden parachute clauses can promise benefits well into the millions. The CEO of Gillette Co., for example, collected $185 million when Procter & Gamble acquired the company. What is more, many golden parachute agreements do not specify that an executive has to perform successfully to be eligible for the award. In a few high-profile cases, executives cashed in their golden parachute while their companies had lost millions of dollars under their stewardship and thousands of employees were laid off. Large parachutes that are awarded once a takeover bid has been announced are particularly suspect; they are little more than going-away presents for the executives and may encourage them to work for the takeover at the expense of the shareholders.

In previous years, it was difficult to ascertain the value of executive severance packages until an executive actually left a company. New SEC executive compensation disclosure rules now require companies to disclose the terms of written or unwritten arrangements that provide payments in case of the resignation, retirement, or termination of the "named executive officers" or the five highest paid executives of a company. The SEC rules also require companies to detail the specific circumstances that would trigger payment and the estimated payment amounts for each situation.

Though this new rule will show whether an executive has an excessive severance package, it does not provide investors with a way to limit them. Congress is considering legislation that will require public companies to hold a nonbinding vote on executive pay plans, including an advisory vote if a company awards a new golden parachute package during a merger, acquisition, or proposed sale.

Despite best efforts to reign in and realign CEO pay, competition for talent keeps driving compensation to higher levels. CEO turnover has reached a record level, both in the United States and abroad, with more than one in seven of the world's 2,500 leading companies making a change in 2005. According to a Lucier, Kocourek, and Habbel (2006), almost half of this turnover involved involuntary dismissals, four times the number a decade ago. The reason for the increase is not entirely clear. One interpretation is that recent reforms are working and that boards—under pressure from shareholders—have become more proactive in firing underperforming CEOs. The survey also shows, however, that CEOs are just as likely to leave prematurely as retire normally, either for a top job at another company or to become a "consultant"—evidence that in many companies the board–CEO relationship still is more adversarial than constructive.

Another factor pushing up compensation is the increasing prevalence of filling CEO openings through external hires rather than through internal promotions. CEOs hired from the outside typically get paid more than CEOs promoted from within. In addition, CEOs in industries with a higher prevalence of outside hiring are paid more than CEOs in industries characterized by internal promotions.[16] The competitive CEO job market also makes retention a more critical issue, further driving up pay, as boards will err on the side of paying more because of the difficulty, disruptiveness, time, and cost associated with finding a replacement.

The growing intensity of the competition for talent is not limited to CEOs. Compensation committees increasingly deal with the compensation demands of second-tier managers, especially CFOs. And even if senior executives are not threatening to leave, base salaries and target levels for bonuses are getting higher because of "benchmarking." Many boards, acting on the advice of compensation consultants, have adopted a policy of setting their CEO's pay above median levels, a practice known among pay critics as the "Lake Wobegon" effect where most every CEO is considered above average.

The Role of the Compensation Committee

The board of directors is responsible for setting CEO pay. Well-designed executive compensation packages are tied to an effective performance evaluation process, reward strong current performance, and provide incentives for creating long-term value. They must be structured to attract, retain, and motivate the right talent, and avoid paying premiums for mediocre or poor performance, or worse, for destroying long-term value. They should be designed to align the interests of management with those of shareholders and other stakeholders in both the short and the long term. While responsibility for CEO performance evaluation (and that of other key senior executives) often rests with the full board, determining appropriate compensation policies for the company's CEO and most senior executives normally is the task of the board's compensation committee.

The role of the compensation committee has changed significantly in recent years. In the wake of the Sarbanes-Oxley legislation, the new SEC rules, and other regulations, many boards are reevaluating the composition, charter, and responsibilities of the compensation committee. This also reflects the fact that the mission of the compensation committee has grown in recent years to include two distinct elements. Strategically, the committee has the responsibility to determine how the achievement of the overall goals and objectives of the company is best supported by specific performance-oriented compensation policies and plans. This includes designing and implementing executive compensation policies aimed at attracting, retaining, and motivating top-flight executives. Administratively, the committee has responsibility for ascertaining that the company's executive compensation programs (covering base salary programs, short- and longer-term incentives, as well as supplemental benefits and perquisites) remain competitive within the market.

Within the context of this expanded mission, compensation committees must

- provide the necessary transparency required by the regulations through proper disclosures within the company's SEC filings;
- recommend for board approval the specific performance criteria and annual and longer term performance targets for awards under the executive compensation program;
- review the performance of the top five officers relative to the achievement of performance objectives for use in calculating award levels under the executive compensation program;
- provide periodic oversight of all short- and long-term incentive plans, perquisites, and other benefits covering the company's executives to ensure that such programs meet the stated performance goals of the organization;
- ensure that all committee business is conducted in a moral and ethical fashion, maintaining the highest levels of personal conduct and professional standards, and taking action to notify the board of any issues—as well as the necessary corrective action— that may affect the committee's ability to objectively fulfill its duties and responsibilities.

Executive Compensation: Best Practices

The challenges facing compensation committees today are formidable. Increased public scrutiny, stronger pressure from shareholders, new regulations, and intense competition for executive talent are causing compensation committees to change their focus beyond providing transparency and compliance to creating value by adopting compensation policies and structures that assist in attracting, developing, and managing executive talent and driving performance.

A review of best practices of companies with a track record of overseeing successful management teams suggest that the most effective compensation committees do the following:

- *Think strategically about executive compensation.* Proactive compensation committees integrate their compensation policies with the company's overall strategy. A move to a new business model, for example, may require different incentives from other growth strategies.

- *Integrate compensation decisions with succession planning.* Very few events have a more dramatic impact on a firm than the unexpected loss of a successful CEO. Winning companies have a succession plan in place that not only addresses "who takes over and when," but also "why" and "how." This requires that the board agrees on the set of skills and competencies needed to execute the company's long-term vision—that is, adopts an objective framework for identifying the right talent to implement the company's chosen strategy.

- *Understand the limitations of benchmarking.* External benchmarking is widely blamed for escalating executive pay levels. Analysis methods should not be blamed, however. The problems arise in their application. Benchmarks can be useful for assessing the competitiveness of compensation packages but should only be considered within the context of performance.

- *Understand how executives view compensation issues.* Executives often take a different perspective from directors in looking at compensation issues. Whereas boards are preoccupied with issues, such as the associated accounting expense, tax consequences, potential share dilution, alignment with the business strategy, and administrative complexity, executives often take a more personal, risk-based perspective.

- *Communicate with major shareholders.* Investors increasingly value an open dialogue about matters, such as potential board nominees or equity grant reserves; their input can give compensation committees a sense of broader shareholder views.

- *Carefully select, monitor, and evaluate their advisers and advisory processes.* NYSE listing standards require boards to evaluate themselves at least annually, and board self-evaluations are quickly becoming a governance best practice. The evaluation process should include the performance of consultants and other outside advisers

CHAPTER 9

Responding to External Pressures and Unforeseen Events

The Rise of Shareholder Activism

In the last 3 decades, individual and institutional shareholders found their voice. Today, they assert their power as a company's owners in many ways—from selling their shares to private or public communication with management and the board, from press campaigns to blogging, from openly talking to other shareholders to putting forward shareholder resolutions, and from calling shareholder meetings to seeking to replace individual directors or the entire board.

Although shareholder proxy proposals typically are not binding or may not receive enough votes to pass, they draw public attention to companies' practices and often force them to reconsider their policies. As a result, a growing number of companies meet with their institutional shareholders during the planning stages of a proposal rather than wait until the implementation stage. And an increasing number of companies are submitting all-equity compensation plans for shareholder approval.

In the United States, the birth of the shareholder rights movement can be traced back to the stock market crash of the late 1920s—investors and policy makers believed this disaster was caused in significant part by companies' lack of transparency. In its aftermath, the Securities and Exchange Commission (SEC) was formed and charged with creating public disclosure and enforcement mechanisms to protect investors and promote the dissemination of reliable corporate information to the marketplace.[1]

In the 1970s, activists' agendas began to include *socially oriented shareholder activism*; religious investors formed a shareholder coalition called the Interfaith Center for Corporate Responsibility (ICCR) and started using the shareholder proposal process as a way of working for peace and social justice. They began organizing and filing resolutions on South African apartheid and community economic development and global finance, environment, equality, international issues, health, and militarism. Today, shareholder resolutions cover a similar range of issues and are used by public interest–minded shareholders and their allies to affect social change on a company level.

Corporate governance activism emerged in the 1980s. This brand of shareholder activism focuses on corporate governance, primarily on how a company structures and compensates its leadership. In 1985, the Council for Institutional Investors (CII) was formed to protect the financial interests of its member investors and pension funds. The CII and its member groups are actively involved in studying and promoting good corporate governance.

One of the most popular shareholder proposals today demands that shareholders be allowed to directly nominate and elect directors rather than work with the slate recommended by the board's nominating committee. Another proposal asks that shareholder resolutions receiving majority support become binding on boards, and that shareholder votes on merger proposals be made mandatory. Support for these further proposals has been lukewarm, however, because they tend to undermine rather than strengthen the role of the board.

In 1989, following the Exxon Valdez disaster, investors and environmentalists banded together to form the Coalition for Environmentally Responsible Economies (CERES), which was built around elements of environmental disclosure. This *investor-environmentalist alliance* uses the power of share ownership to persuade companies to adopt a set of environmental principles and produce public, standardized, annual, environmental reports.

Today, shareholder resolutions are used more than ever as a way of influencing corporate behavior and concern issues ranging from corporate political contributions to health care, from executive compensation to board leadership, and from the environment to animal welfare.

Institutional shareholders, especially hedge funds, are a major force behind these developments. Using the power of activism to influence policies at companies in which they have significant holdings, they have begun to scrutinize stock plan dilution, compensation practices, and merger proposals. Mutual fund firms, which have traditionally not been vocal on behalf of shareholder rights, are getting more involved. And more institutions are turning to their most powerful form of activism and voting "no" on key items.

A contributing factor is the short-term boost such efforts can have on stock prices. Thomson Financial studied the performance of stock in 75 companies targeted by activist investors—whether hedge funds, public pension funds, or other entities—between 2001 and 2006. Within the first 3 months of being publicly targeted, the companies on average saw their shares rise nearly 12%, well above the rise of less than 1.5% for a control group of stocks. After one year, the 75 companies posted gains of 17%, compared to a rise of 7.2% in the control group.[2]

Not surprisingly, shareholder activism is controversial. Proponents argue that companies with active and engaged shareholders are more likely to be successful in the long term than those that largely function on their own. In their view, vigilant shareholders act as fire alarms, and their mere presence helps alleviate managerial or boardroom complacency. Opponents say that "shareholder activism" is a form of disruptive, uninformed, populist meddling that encourages short-term behavior and diverts a board from a focus on value creation. Some particularly worry about the rise of hedge-fund activism. They note that although hedge funds hold great promise as active shareholders, their intense involvement in corporate governance and control also potentially raises a major problem, namely, that the interests of hedge funds sometimes diverge from those of their fellow shareholders. These polar opposites reflect the broader societal disagreement about how much power shareholders should delegate to corporate boards and when direct shareholder action becomes necessary and on what terms.

Demands for Corporate Social Responsibility (CSR)

Most of the pressure on boards in the last 25 years has come from shareholders. More recently, however, a different source of pressure—the demand for *corporate social responsibility* (CSR)—has emerged, which is forcing directors into new governance territory occupied by stakeholders other than shareholders. While pressure on corporate executives to pay greater attention to stakeholder concerns and make CSR an integral part of corporate strategy has been mounting since the early 1990s, such pressure is only now beginning to filter through to the board.

The emergence of CSR as a more prominent item on a board's agenda reflects a shift in popular opinion about the role of business in society and the convergence of environmental forces, such as the following:

- *Globalization.* There are now more than 60,000 multinational corporations estimated to be in the world.[3] Perceptions about the growing reach and influence of global companies has drawn attention to the impact of business on society. This has led to heightened demands for corporations to take responsibility for the social, environmental, and economic effects of their actions. It has also spawned more aggressive demands for corporations to set their sights on limiting harm and actively seeking to improve social, economic, and environmental circumstances.
- *Loss of trust.* High-profile cases of corporate financial misdeeds (Enron, WorldCom, and others) and of social and environmental irresponsibility (e.g., Shell's alleged complicity in political repression in Nigeria; Exxon's oil spill in Prince William Sound in Alaska; Nike's and other apparel makers' links with "sweatshop" labor in developing countries; questions about Nestlé's practices in marketing baby formula in the developing world) have contributed to a broad-based decline in trust in corporations and corporate leaders. The public's growing reluctance to give corporations the benefit of the doubt has led to intensified scrutiny of corporate impact on society, the economy, and the environment, and a greater readiness to assume—rightly or wrongly—immoral corporate intent.

- *Civil society activism.* The growing activity and sophistication of "civil society" organizations, many of which are oriented to social and environmental causes, has generated pressure on corporations to take CSR seriously.[4] Well-known international nongovernmental organizations (NGOs), such as Oxfam, Amnesty International, Greenpeace, the Rainforest Action Network, and the Fair Labor Association, have influenced corporate decision making in areas, such as access to essential medicines, labor standards, environmental protection, and human rights. The advent of the Internet has increased the capacity of these organizations—as well as a plethora of national and local civic associations—to monitor corporate behavior and mobilize public opinion.[5]
- *Institutional investor interest in CSR.* The growth in "socially responsible investing" has created institutional demand for equity in corporations that demonstrate a commitment to CSR. Recent growth in assets involved in socially responsible investing has outpaced growth in all professionally managed investment assets in the United States, even though the mainstream financial community has been slow to incorporate nonfinancial factors into its analyses of corporate value.[6]

These trends indicate that there is both a growing perception that corporations must be more accountable to society for their actions, and a growing willingness and capacity within society to impose accountability on corporations. This has profound implications for the future of corporate governance. It suggests that boards will soon have to deal with

- a growing pressure to give stakeholders a role in corporate governance;
- a growing pressure on corporations to disclose more and better information about their management of social, environmental, and economic issues;
- an increasing level of regulatory compulsion related to elements of corporate activity that are currently regarded as voluntary forms of social responsibility;

- a growing interest by the mainstream financial community in the link between shareholder value and nonfinancial corporate performance.

The discussion about corporate accountability to stakeholders, therefore, while often couched in the vocabulary of CSR, is really a discussion about the changing definition of corporate governance, which is why it should receive a greater priority on the board's agenda.

Interestingly, whereas board agendas mostly focus on competition, cooperation may well become the preferred business strategy for addressing social and environmental issues. Increasingly, companies are joining forces not only with business competitors but also with human rights and environmental activists (formerly considered enemies), as well as socially responsible investors, academics, and governmental organizations. At the 2007 World Economic Forum (WEF) gathering, for example, two such coalitions were announced to address the issue of global online freedom of expression, particularly in repressive regimes. One, facilitated by Business for Social Responsibility (BSR), consists of companies facing intense criticism over complicity with suppressing online free speech in China. This coalition includes big names, such as Google, Microsoft, and Yahoo. The other gathered together socially responsible investing firms and human rights advocates, such as Amnesty International, Human Rights Watch, and Reporters Without Borders.

Dealing With Hostile Takeovers

Corporate takeovers became a prominent feature of the U.S. business landscape during the 1970s and 1980s. Hostile acquisitions generally involve poorly performing firms in mature industries and occur when the board of directors of the target is opposed to the sale of the company. In this case, the acquiring firm has two options to proceed with the acquisition—a tender offer or a proxy fight.

Tender Offers and Proxy Fights

A *tender offer* represents an offer to buy the stock of the target firm either directly from the firm's shareholders or through the secondary market. The purchaser typically offers a premium price to encourage the shareholders to sell their shares. The offer has a time limit, and it may have other provisions that the target company must abide by if shareholders accept the offer. The bidding company must disclose its plans for the target company and file with the SEC. Sometimes, a purchaser or group of purchasers will gradually buy up enough stock to gain a controlling interest (known as a creeping tender offer), without making a public tender offer. This is risky because the target company could discover the attempted takeover and take steps to prevent it.

Because it allows bidders to seek control directly from shareholders—by going "over the heads" of target management—the tender offer is the most powerful weapon available to the hostile bidder. Indeed, just the threat of a hostile tender offer can often bring a recalcitrant target management to the bargaining table, especially if the bidder already owns a substantial block of the target's stock and can demonstrably afford to finance a hostile offer for control. Although hostile bidders still need a formal agreement to gain total control of the target's assets, this is often easily accomplished once the bidder has purchased a majority of voting stock.

When there are strong differences between a board and a company's shareholders about the firm's long-term strategy, its executive compensation policies, or a merger or acquisition proposal, a *proxy fight* is likely to ensue. This occurs when the board sends out its proxy statement in which it seeks shareholder approval for a variety of actions. Proxy contests are usually waged to replace members of the board of directors, but they can also be used to gain support in other efforts like an acquisition. They tend to involve publicly traded companies but can also target closed-end mutual funds.

A leveraged buyout (LBO) is a variation of a hostile takeover. In an LBO, the buyer borrows heavily to pay for the acquisition, either from traditional bank loans or through high-yield (junk) bonds. This can be risky, since incurring so much debt can seriously harm the value of the acquiring company.

Defense Mechanisms

The management and directors of target firms may resist takeover attempts either to get a higher price for the firm or to protect their own self-interests. The most effective methods are built-in defensive measures that make a company difficult to take over. These methods are collectively referred to as "shark repellent." Here are a few examples:

- A *golden parachute*, or change-of-control agreement, is an agreement that provides key executives with generous severance pay and other benefits in the event that their employment is terminated as a result of a change of ownership of the company. Golden parachutes are voted on by the board of directors and, depending on the laws of the state in which the company is incorporated, may require shareholder approval. Some golden parachutes are triggered even if the control of the corporation does not change completely; such parachutes open after a certain percentage of the corporation's stock is acquired.
- The *supermajority* is a defense that requires 70% or 80% of shareholders to approve of any acquisition. This makes it much more difficult for someone to conduct a takeover by buying enough stock for a controlling interest.
- A *staggered* board of directors drags out the takeover process by preventing the entire board from being replaced at the same time. The terms are staggered, so that some members are elected every 2 years, while others are elected every 4 years. Many companies that are interested in making an acquisition are not willing to wait 4 years for the board to turn over.
- *Dual-class* stock allows company owners to hold onto voting stock, while the company issues stock with little or no voting rights to the public. This allows investors to purchase stock, but they cannot purchase control of the company.
- With a *Lobster Trap* strategy, the company passes a provision preventing anyone with more than 10% ownership from converting convertible securities into voting stock. Examples of convertible securities include convertible bonds, convertible preferred stock, and warrants.

In addition to preventing a takeover, there are steps boards can take to thwart a takeover once the process has begun. One of the more common defenses is the adoption of a so-called *poison pill*. Poison pills can take many forms and refer to anything the target company does to make itself less valuable or less desirable as an acquisition. Some examples include the following:

- *A legal challenge.* The target company may file suit against the bidder alleging violations of antitrust or securities laws.
- *The people pill.* High-level managers and other employees threaten that they will all leave the company if it is acquired. This only works if the employees themselves are highly valuable and vital to the company's success.
- *Asset or liability restructuring.* With asset restructuring, the target purchases assets that the bidder does not want or that will create antitrust problems, or sells off the assets that the suitor desires to obtain. The so-called *Crown Jewel* defense is an example. Sometimes a specific aspect of a company is particularly valuable. A pharmaceutical company might have a highly regarded research and development (R&D) division—a crown jewel. It might respond to a hostile bid by selling off the R&D division to another company, or spinning it off into a separate corporation. Liability restructuring maneuvers include the so-called *Macaroni defense*—an approach by which a target company issues a large number of bonds with the condition that they must be redeemed at a high price if the company is taken over. Why is it called a Macaroni defense? Because if a company is in danger, the redemption price of the bonds expands like macaroni in a pot! Issuing shares to a friendly third party—the so-called *White Knight* defense—to dilute the bidder's ownership position is another often-used tactic. In rare cases, a company decides that it would rather go out of business than be acquired, so they intentionally accumulate enough debt to force bankruptcy. This is known as the *Jonestown defense*.
- *Flip-in.* This common poison pill is a provision that allows current shareholders to buy more stock at a steep discount in the

event of a takeover attempt. The provision is often triggered whenever any one shareholder reaches a certain percentage of total shares (usually 20% to 40%). This dilutes the value of the stock; it also reduces voting power because each share becomes a smaller percentage of the total

- *Greenmail.* Greenmail is defined as an action in which the target company repurchases the shares of an unfriendly suitor at a premium over the current market price.
- *The Pac-Man Defense.* A target company thwarts a takeover by buying stock in the acquiring company, then launching a takeover.

Despite the seemingly obvious advantages, takeover defenses of all kinds lately have become the target of increasingly potent shareholder activism. The primary shareholder complaints against poison pills are that they entrench management and the board and discourage legitimate tender offers. Institutional Shareholder Services (ISS; now part of Risk-Metrics Group), an influential provider of proxy voting and corporate governance services, recommends that institutions vote in favor of shareholder proposals requesting that the company submit its poison pill or any future pills to a shareholder vote, or redeem poison pills already in existence. In addition, a company that has a poison pill in place that has not been approved by shareholders will suffer a significant downgrading in the ISS's ratings system. Today, about one third of the Standard & Poor's 500 companies continue to have poison pills.

Shareholder proposals requesting the company to submit its poison pill or any future pills to a shareholder vote, or to terminate an existing poison pill, are not binding on a board—even if overwhelmingly approved by the shareholders. However, if a company fails to implement a proposal approved by the shareholders, there likely will be significant negative consequences for the company and its incumbent directors, including the perception that the company is not responsive to the wishes of its shareholders, substantial withholding of votes in director elections, and downgraded corporate governance ratings.

The Board's Role in Crisis Management[7]

Crises are inevitable. Large corporations can expect to face a crisis on average every 4 to 5 years. Every CEO will probably have to manage at least one crisis during his or her tenure. A director may have to face two or three crises during a normal tour of service on a board. Crises can take many forms—an industrial accident, product tampering, financial improprieties, sexual harassment allegations, or a hostile takeover. Any sudden event that threatens a company's financial performance, reputation, or its relations with key stakeholders has the potential to become a crisis.

Some crises are preventable, others are not. Many are of a company's own making, resulting from sins of commission or omission. In those cases, the board certainly has a role to play in crisis prevention and has clear accountability for failing to faithfully execute its fiduciary duties. A good many crises begin as problems, developing gradually over time, with plenty of opportunities for an alert board to step in and take corrective action.

Nadler (2004) groups crises into one of four categories:

1. *Gradual emergence, external origin.* These might involve economic downturns or the emergence of competitive threats, such as breakthrough technologies, new go-to-market strategies, alliances of major competitors, or regulatory changes that limit business practices or expand competition.
2. *Gradual emergence, internal origin.* Examples range from strategic mistakes (such as a poorly conceived merger) to failed product launches, the loss of key talent to competitors, and employee discrimination suits.
3. *Abrupt emergence, external origin.* Some of the most obvious examples are natural disasters, terrorist attacks, and product tampering.
4. *Abrupt emergence, internal origin.* This can include the sudden death or resignation of one or more key executives, failure of critical technology, production, or delivery systems, or the discovery of fraud.

In the event of a gradually emerging crisis, a carefully designed risk-management process should provide warnings, in plenty of time, for the company either to avoid the problem entirely or to take corrective action before it develops into a full-blown crisis. Abrupt crises are more problematic; no one can predict a terrorist attack, an earthquake, a plane crash, a shooting spree by a disgruntled employee, or a CEO's sudden decision to quit and go to work for a competitor. But sound planning can help the company mitigate the consequences and speed the recovery. The board has an obligation to ensure that management regularly reviews, updates, and practices all aspects of crisis planning.

To deal effectively with any of these scenarios, a board must put together its own crisis-management plan, which identifies the different roles it may have to play depending on management's role in the crisis. The most challenging situation occurs when the CEO is the source of the crisis. This scenario requires identifying what specific role board leaders and individual directors should play, and who the board should call on for independent guidance on legal, financial, or public relations issues.[8]

Thus, the board needs to be absolutely clear about how it will be organized during a crisis, which members have particular expertise it can call upon, and who will take the lead in efforts to restore the confidence of employees, investors, and other stakeholders.

Crises Involving the CEO

During most crises, the board has an important but secondary role to play. That is, ordinarily the CEO is the chief crisis manager and communicator, and the board operates in the background to provide oversight, advice, and support. But, as noted above, when the CEO is the cause of the crisis, the board has no choice but to assume the full burden of safeguarding the interests of the company and its shareholders. That situation can arise for a host of reasons. The most obvious is the CEO's death or sudden departure.

To determine who should take the lead in the event of a crisis, the board first must decide whether the crisis creates a real or potential conflict between the interests of management and the company. A hostile takeover bid, for example, may threaten the jobs of senior executives but still be in the best interests of shareholders. In such instances, only the board can provide the necessary leadership to maintain stability in the company and retain the confidence of employees, customers, and investors.

Every board should have a detailed plan for dealing with the sudden and unexpected loss of the CEO. Once emergency succession plans for the CEO and other top officers have been developed and agreed on by the board and the CEO, they should be reviewed and updated at least once a year.

Other Crises: The Board's Role in Supporting and Advising the CEO

Most corporate crises are not about the CEO. Usually, therefore, the CEO will act as the chief crisis officer with the board playing a supporting role—approving key decisions, providing the CEO with a confidential sounding board, giving informed advice based on directors' previous crisis experience or special expertise, and demonstrating confidence in the CEO and support for management's efforts to navigate the crisis.

In a crisis, boards need two things above all else: information and a credible, candid communications policy that keeps shareholders, the media, and everybody else abreast of what is happening. If necessary, boards should launch an independent investigation of what happened and why, and retain their own outside counsel. Constant communication between the CEO and the board is also critical. The CEO must keep the board informed as events unfold and should engage the board in evaluating alternative courses of action. This provides the CEO with the benefit of the board's collective experience with crises at other companies.

Recovery and Learning

After a crisis, the opportunity for collective introspection and improvement is brief because there is an inevitable push to regain normalcy, calm, and control. This is when the board should demonstrate its independence, leadership, and value to the organization by insisting that management stop and learn the most important lessons from its brush with disaster. It also is an opportune time to review, evaluate, and update the organization's capabilities in the areas of risk assessment, crisis planning, and organizational recovery.[9]

The bottom line is that, in quieter times, boards could conduct their affairs in a climate of privacy and anonymity. Today, directors are increasingly exposed to all kinds of pressures—from the government, regulatory agencies, shareholders, NGOs, the press, consumers, and ordinary citizens. To deal with this heightened level of public scrutiny, boards must learn to function effectively in an environment of openness and transparency, and learn how to respond to such pressures and to unexpected events.

CHAPTER 10

Creating a High-Performance Board

Managing Itself: A Board's First Priority

A strong and effective board is clear about its role in relationship to management and understands the difference between managing and governing. A board's principal duty is to provide oversight; management's duty is to run the company. A good board also understands that it, not management, has ultimate responsibility for directing the company's affairs as defined by law.

To meet these obligations, a board must take responsibility for its own agenda, or it will not be independent. Management cannot be responsible for directors' skills and processes and should not have more than a consultative role in decisions, such as choosing new directors. Boards can no longer be just "advisers" who wait for management to come to them. As fiduciaries, they must be active monitors of management.

The specifics of the board's role and modus operandi will vary with size, the stage and strategy of the company, and the talents and personalities of the CEO and the board. Clearly, "one size does not fit all." There are, however, basic legal requirements and "management" skills that boards can and should adopt regardless of their role and structure. The goal should be to *make the board perform as well as it wants the company managed.*

Two critical determinants of board effectiveness are the directors' individual and collective *motivation* and *capabilities*. The most effective boards score high on both dimensions; they know and respect the difference between governance and management and appreciate where and when they can add value. Conversely, boards that score low on both dimensions are likely to be ineffective and function mainly as a statutory body. Capable boards with low levels of motivation represent a missed opportunity, whereas highly motivated but less capable boards tend to meddle or micromanage.

What Defines the Best In-Class Boards?

What makes for a good board? In *Building High-Performance Boards*, executive search consultants Heidrick & Struggles observe that a high-performance board governs by continually challenging—in a positive way—every significant aspect of the company's operations: its business model, strategies, and underlying assumptions; its operating performance; and its leadership development. In doing so, a best in-class board should seek to create a culture of rigorous, relentless examination, and press for continuous improvement. This way it can set a "tone at the top" that reverberates throughout the organization—to employees, to customers, to shareholders, and to the communities served by the company. A best in-class board, therefore, is more than a roster of prominent names; it is a well-balanced team that leverages the diverse experiences, skills, and intellects of the directors to further the strategic objectives of the company. Members of such boards focus on the big picture yet know when to drill down on specifics; they have the fortitude to speak openly and candidly, and the humility to remember that they do not run the business. Thus, being a good director is both a skill and a mindset.[1]

A recent study by Bird, Buchanan, and Rogers (2004) for Bain & Company concludes that truly effective boards concentrate on value growth and practice seven habits that build their effectiveness:[2]

1. *Effective boards own the strategy.* Strong boards contribute to strategic thinking and feel a sense of ownership of the resulting strategy itself. The authors cite the case of Vodafone, where each year the board helps develop the agenda for a multi-day strategy retreat with senior executives. Each director contributes to the list of key strategic decisions that need to be made at the retreat. The event begins with a highly analytic overview of Vodafone's markets and competitors, providing data that will inform those decisions. Instead of just including presentations by executives to the board, Vodafone's

process fosters debate on options, investments, and returns. When boards understand the issues at this depth and ask critical questions early on—Is the strategy bold enough? Is it achievable?—they can respond more quickly to opportunities such as major acquisitions when they arise. Decisions unfold faster. Vodafone's swift consummation of the Mannesmann acquisition aptly demonstrates the value of such an approach.[3]

2. *Effective boards build the top team.* As noted in earlier chapters, selecting, developing, and evaluating the top executive team are major board responsibilities. A truly effective board understands the significance of developing leaders to creating market value, and therefore has a strong incentive to get involved. Yet, Bain & Company's analysis of 23 high-growth companies revealed that only a minority systematically try to develop new leadership through internal advancement.

3. *Effective boards link reward to performance.* Determining the right reward structure starts with how the company chooses to measure success—and how closely these measures are tied to the drivers of long-term value in the business, not with pay systems. Selecting the right approach is critical, because CEO compensation remains a controversial issue for many companies. Effective compensation schemes measure what matters and pay for performance, with a real downside for mediocre results. They also are simple and transparent and focus on sustained value creation, balancing short-term and long-term focus.

4. *Effective boards focus on financial viability.* As noted in earlier chapters, ensuring a company's financial viability extends well beyond complying with the Sarbanes-Oxley Act and other applicable laws. It includes making other key financial decisions, such as choosing appropriate levels of debt and scrutinizing major investments and acquisition proposals. As Bird, Buchanan, and Rogers observe, worst practices can sometimes be instructive. They cite an investigation by former U.S. Attorney General Richard Thornburgh into WorldCom's $11 billion in accounting irregularities that concluded that WorldCom's directors were often kept in the dark, particularly in matters involving some of the company's more than 60 acquisitions.

The study also revealed that the company's directors made little effort to monitor debt levels or the company's ability to repay obligations; yet, they "rubber-stamped" proposals by WorldCom's senior executives to increase borrowings.

5. *Effective companies match risk with return.* Most boards have a process in place for assessing and managing operational risk. Yet, as noted in chapter 6 in the section on enterprise risk management, few boards understand the true risks inherent in their companies' strategies. This is critical: Almost three quarters of major acquisitions destroy rather than create value, and 70% of diversification efforts away from the core business and into new markets fail. Furthermore, Bain & Company estimates that more than 40% of recent CEO departures not related to retirement can be attributed to a controversial or failed "adjacency" move. The message: Boards need to understand and accept the risks inherent in their strategy and recognize the implications for required risk-weighted returns.

6. *Effective boards manage corporate reputation.* Strong boards avoid the traps of "check-the-box" compliance and a short-term horizon; they target long-term value creation and ignore guidance by "analysts" and court investors who seek long-term value. Once a course is set, they focus on transparency and effective communication to enhance their reputation.

7. *Effective boards manage themselves.* An effective board chair sets the tone from the top and implements an effective governance model. Such a model (a) focuses the agenda on issues of performance and regularly reviews board effectiveness, (b) builds a team of directors with the right mix of skills and experience, and (c) is clear about the value a board can contribute, and (d) ensures that directors have ample opportunities to fulfill their roles.

The Right Leadership: The Key to Board Effectiveness

Independent board leadership capable of shepherding the board's priorities and providing a voice for the concerns of other outside directors is critical to board effectiveness. While not the only way to establish such leadership, a nonexecutive chair can strengthen the independence of the board and help create a healthy check-and-balance between management and the board. As an alternative, some boards have adopted the so-called lead director model. If they do choose to appoint a nonexecutive chair, boards should ensure that the individual selected for this position has the experience, temperament, and commitment to the role to be effective. An effective chair serves as the leader of the board, keeps directors focused on the board's major priorities, sets meeting agendas, leads discussions, and occasionally serves as a board spokesperson. According to consulting firm Spencer Stuart, the chair's specific responsibilities cover four main areas:

1. *Managing the board.* This involves chairing board meetings, as well as leading executive sessions of the independent directors.
2. *Communication.* This includes maintaining regular communications with senior management and other directors to set meeting agendas and to discuss information flow and emerging issues.
3. *Succession planning.* Nonexecutive chairs are well positioned to play a leading role in CEO succession planning.
4. *Board evaluations.* Best practice suggests that the governance committee should manage the board and director evaluation process, with the committee chair gathering director feedback. Nevertheless, the chair has a significant role to play in conflict resolution.[4]

In addition to being a focal point for the board, the chair can also be an important mentor for the CEO. Many people, therefore, believe he or she should be a consensus choice of both the board members and the CEO. Also, as part of his or her duties, a chair should make him- or herself visible inside the company—by participating in major company meetings, by being easily accessible to employees (in person, via e-mail, or by phone). The rationale for creating visibility is that, if bad things happen in the company, employees should know they have a person on the board—namely the chair—they can go to.

Performing all these duties well is a tall order and requires a unique combination of experience, dedication, and the right temperament. To lead effectively, a nonexecutive chair must understand the function of each board committee and the role of an individual director, and must be conscious of not undermining the CEO's authority, especially in front of the senior management team. Learning on the job is not an option.

Beyond executive and board experience, good "people" and "communication" skills are essential. A nonexecutive chair must know how to create focus and how to build consensus on the board. He or she also needs to facilitate effective communication between the board and management and avoid becoming a barrier between the two. This requires diplomacy, an ability to be direct and concise without offending anyone, a passion for the job, and a minimal ego. An effective nonexecutive chair exercises leadership and avoids creating the impression that he or she is trying to run the show.

Who can fill these rather large shoes? According to Spencer Stuart, 73% of the nonexecutive chairs on Standard & Poor's 500 boards are retired corporate executives. About half formerly served as the CEO of another company—experience that is extremely valuable to be effective in the role.[5]

Understanding the "Sociology" of the Board

A board's primary role is a fiduciary one. It is not surprising, therefore, that most board processes are designed with this objective in mind—to ensure management is accountable to the board and the board to shareholders. Recent reforms also reflect this bias toward the fiduciary role of the board. Consider, for example, the focus on greater disclosure, director independence, executive sessions, increased communications with major shareholders, and on separating the offices of chairman and CEO. All these changes are aimed at providing greater transparency and increased accountability. They do not, however, address the deeper issue of how the board can function better as a group.

No group can operate effectively without a well-defined, shared understanding of its primary role and accountability. The ongoing debate about the fundamental purpose and accountability of the modern corporation has created a problem for boards as a whole, as well as for individual directors—what behaviorists call a heightened sense of role ambiguity and, in some instances, increased role conflict. For example, while recent regulatory reforms promote enhanced transparency and accountability, they also may well increase directors' anxiety about their ability to effectively carry out their responsibilities to say nothing about their personal

exposure to legal and other challenges. If true, the outcome may be opposite of what is intended—a decrease in proactive conduct and more conservative "defensive" behavior on the part of directors, individually and as
a group. And while recent reforms may clarify some of the formal rules
that govern board composition and operation, little attention has been
paid to what impact these changes are likely to have on the unstated or
informal rules that govern much of actual board behavior.

Formal Versus Informal Rules

All group behavior, including that of boards, is governed by formal and
informal rules. Formal rules include explicit policies about how often
they meet, how they structure their meetings, who participates on what
committees, and how issues are decided by discussion and vote. As with
many groups, however, board behavior is also governed by a set of powerful unstated informal rules or norms. For example, asking management
"tough, penetrating" questions about performance is formally encouraged and seen as part of a director's duty. At the same time, if a director
pursues an issue too long or too vigorously, he or she may be seen to violate any one of a number of unstated rules about what the other directors
consider "effective" board membership.[6]

This is one explanation for why so many boardroom votes are unani-
mous. While it is acceptable to occasionally cast a dissenting vote, if a
board member repeatedly votes "against" his or her peers, however, he
or she may be asked whether he or she is "for" or "against" management,
and whether he or she has a hidden agenda. Norms also influence individual behavior after the group has reached a decision. For example, many
boards operate under an unstated rule that directors should not criticize
or reexamine the board's past decisions.

What happens when a director violates an unstated norm? While the
consequences for breaching formal board rules are fairly clear, the punish-
ment for violating informal rules is less well defined. Because informal
rules are implicit, corrective action primarily takes the form of exercising "peer" pressure. Since directors generally do not interact very much
outside the boardroom, any exercise of corrective peer pressure is mainly
confined to the boardroom itself, and therefore governed by the board's

prevailing set of group norms. What is more, since directors do not have the power to directly remove ineffective or confrontational peers, the scope of such corrective action is limited. And, unless the breach is so disruptive that he has no alternative, the chair, especially if he is also the CEO, will likely hesitate before confronting the offending director.

These two factors—the difficulty directors have discussing, questioning, or reconsidering the appropriateness of various norms and their uncertainty about the repercussions of breaching formal or informal rules—also explain why boards have tended to search "among their own"—that is, other CEOs with board experience—for new directors. Potentially embarrassing problems can be avoided when boards choose candidates who likely already understand the "rules," especially the informal norms, that govern board conduct.[7]

Group Influences on Individual Behavior

It is well known that individuals behave differently in groups than they behave when they are alone. In a group, much of our individual behavior is determined by the behavior of other group members. In a board setting, this raises an important question: What happens when an individual director's beliefs and opinions differ from those of the other members of the group? Does he vote according to his conscience, or will he likely compromise and vote with the majority in the face of real or perceived peer pressure? This dilemma occurs more often than one might think. Consider the following questions directors routinely face: Should I go along with the compensation committee's recommendation for a substantial increase for the the CEO even though, deep down, I believe he is already paid too much? Do I vote "no" on the aggressive debt restructuring proposal when other members of the board clearly are for the proposal? How do I act when a senior board member who has mentored me before pulls me aside and urges me to go along with the majority for the sake of "unity" on the board? As these questions illustrate, group norms do not only strongly influence individual behavior—they may even dictate what perceptions, beliefs, and judgments are deemed appropriate. It is not surprising, therefore, that new board members often accept the judgment of more senior directors and choose to vote with them. This also explains why the current focus on director independence may well be misplaced; it has little or no relation to the underlying sociological issues that shape board behavior.

The above examples also illustrate how the presence of other more experienced and powerful group members can discourage individuals from participating up to their full potential. Sociologists label this phenomenon "social inhibition." It is expressed in several different behaviors: loafing (i.e., minimizing effort while hiding behind the work of others), self-handicapping (e.g., knowingly accepting a very difficult challenge to avoid the risk of failing at a simple task), or conforming simply to get along. All of these behaviors can be found in the boardroom, and all must explicitly be addressed to create a high performance board.

Time and Information Deficits: Barriers to Board Effectiveness

To carry out their responsibilities, directors need to know a great deal. They must be knowledgeable about the company's financial results, its competitive position, its customers, its products, its technologies, and the capabilities of its workforce; they must be aware of the performance and challenges of its top executives, as well as the depth and readiness of its broader talent pool. Boards also need to review information about the culture of the organization and about how customers and employees feel about the company. Finally, boards must closely monitor the company's compliance with legal, regulatory, and ethical standards. Because of a board's time constraints, the only effective approach is for the board to focus on lead indicators. The challenge is to know what the right lead indicators are—that is, which ones are unique to the company and its business model.

Available time is a major issue. Outside, independent board members usually hold significant leadership positions in their own organizations making it difficult for them to spend a large amount of time on board matters. Another is the inadequacy of the information provided to directors. Directors typically receive (a) operating statements, balance sheets, and statements of cash flow that compare current period and year-to-date results to plan and last year, (b) management comments about the foregoing that explain the reasons for variations from plan and provide a revised forecast of results for the remainder of the year, (c) share of market information, (d) minutes of prior board and some management committee meetings, (e) selected documents on the company, its products and services and competition, (f) financial analyst's reports for the company and sometimes for major competitors, and (g) on an ad hoc basis, special information, such as consultants reports, customer preference data, or employee attitude surveys. A strong argument can be made that this is no longer enough, particularly in fast-changing industries and in companies with an increasingly global reach. Questions, such as, Are we going in the right direction? Are management's assumptions about major trends and changes correct? Is the company doing the critical things to get the job done? Should our strategy be changed? cannot be answered meaningfully on the basis of mostly historical information or with summaries of proposed actions.

Dashboards and Scorecards

Originally created for CEOs, CFOs, and heads of business units to monitor hundreds of key financial, sales, and operational details, dashboards and scorecards are increasingly being introduced to the boardroom. Major companies whose boards use some form of dashboards include General Electric, Home Depot, and Microsoft.[8]

Web-based dashboards and their less sophisticated predecessors, scorecards, can display critical information in easy-to-understand charts and graphics on a timely basis. The most sophisticated dashboards allow users to drill down for additional details. For example, to diagnose a negative cash-flow trend, a director can quickly probe whether the shortfall is due to a receivables problem or the result of excessive spending.

A major advantage of dashboards is that they can be tailored to specific needs. Of course, any director dashboard should have a basic menu of common information, such as financial, sales, and compliance-related data. Beyond this common format, however, the configuration of the dashboard can be tailored to responsibilities of a particular director; an audit committee member might want special information on the subject of fraud prevention and detection, for example. Other examples include the ability of a director who serves on the compensation committee to immediately see whose options have been exercised, or an audit committee director's up-to-the-minute update on Sarbanes-Oxley compliance progress.

Direct communication channels are also important. Directors should have access to top management other than the CEO. Effective boards have protocols in place that allow a director, with permission of the board chair and CEO, to speak directly with employees. Conversely, directors need to be accessible to management and employees of the organization.[9]

Board Access to External Advisers

The board and board committees should, as needed, retain external experts, such as counsel, consultants, and other expert professionals, and investigate any issues they believe should be examined to fulfill the board's duty of care. These external experts and consultants should have a direct line of communication and reporting responsibility to the board and not management.

Building the Right Team: Board Composition[1]

The composition of the board should be tailored to the needs of the company. The board of an acquisitive company, for example, should be well represented with deal-making expertise and judgement, while the directors of a fast-moving technology company need a sound view of the industry's future direction. However, every board needs to have certain essential ingredients, with the individual directors possessing knowledge in core areas, such as accounting and finance, technology, management, marketing, international operations, and industry knowledge. The best directors enrich their board with the perspective of someone who has faced some of the same problems that the company may face in the future. In addition, organizations in the early stages of building—or rebuilding—a boardroom culture, often are best served by a knowledgeable, forceful advocate for exemplary corporate governance.

Behavioral characteristics are a major determinant of board effectiveness. Effective directors do not hesitate to ask the hard questions, work well with others, understand the industry, provide valuable input, are available when needed, are alert and inquisitive, have relevant business knowledge, contribute to committee work, attend meetings regularly, speak out appropriately at board meetings, prepare for meetings, and make meaningful contributions.

The NYSE recommends that director qualification standards be included in the company's corporate governance guidelines. Companies sometimes include other substantive qualifications, such as policies limiting the number of other boards on which a director may serve and director tenure, retirement, and succession. The chairman of the nominating committee should certify in the proxy that the committee has reviewed the qualifications of each director—both standing for election and on the board generally. Finally, every director should receive appropriate training, including his or her duties as a director when he or she is first appointed to the board. This should include an orientation-training program to ensure that incoming directors are familiar with the company's business and governance practices. Equally important, directors should receive ongoing training, particularly on relevant new laws, regulations, and changing commercial risks, as needed.

Board Self-Evaluation[2]

In the aftermath of Sarbanes-Oxley, the stock exchanges mandated that boards of public companies and key committees, such as the audit committee, evaluate their own performance annually. Since there is no mandated or standard approach for such an evaluation, boards should select a process that best fits their needs. At a minimum, the director performance evaluation process should ensure that each director meets the board's qualifications for membership when the director is nominated or renominated to the board. Evaluation of the board and committees should also determine whether each has fulfilled its basic, required functions.

In designing a suitable process, questions, such as, Why are we doing this? What areas do we need to focus on? How can we receive valid feedback? How can we act on that feedback to make a difference? Where can we find the required expertise, internally and externally? Who do we want to handle, analyze, and provide feedback to the board? To the chairman or lead director? To the CEO? To committees? To individual directors? must first be answered.

Many boards are not sufficiently aware of the type of expertise that is available to assist them in board evaluation and development. As a result, they may overestimate their own capabilities in this area and underestimate the value of external resources. One place for boards to turn is their internal or external counsel. A number of law firms are broadening their scope of service to include board evaluation. This makes sense in a litigious environment where the fear of shareholder lawsuits has arisen and where directors may be worried that the information revealed in a board evaluation process may make them more vulnerable. Retaining legal counsel to perform the evaluation may reduce this fear by having counsel assert privilege over such matters. However, even without legal privilege being asserted by counsel over the evaluation process and its documents, courts are likely to have a more favorable view of a board that chooses to take a tough look at how it can do better, documents the process intelligently, and acts on what it finds rather than one that does not evaluate itself at all.

Others may bring more important skills to the table. For example, professionals in industrial and organizational psychology often have relevant training. Depending upon a board's likelihood of being involved in litigation, it may be advisable to ask external counsel to work collaboratively with external experts specializing in board and director performance effectiveness.

While there is no single, best approach to board evaluation, best practice suggests that an effective board and director evaluation process is (a) *controlled by the board itself*—not by management or outside consultants; (b) *confidential and collegial*—it should foster an atmosphere of candor and trust; (c) *led by a champion*—alternatives include the non-CEO chairman, the lead independent director or equivalent, or the chair of the nominating and governance committee; and (d) *focused on identifying areas of improvement*—in areas such as creating a balance of power between the board and management, focusing the board more on long-term strategy, more effectively fulfilling the board's oversight responsibilities, the adequacy of committee structures, and updating the evaluation process itself.

A good process also *evaluates individual director performance*—through self-assessment and peer review. This should include consideration of independence, level of contribution, and attendance; take specific board roles into account; and provide a basis for determining the suitability of a director's reelection.

PART III

The Future

EPILOGUE

The Future of Corporate Governance

About Epilogues

The *Encarta Dictionary* defines an *epilogue* as "a short Chapter or Section at the end of a literary work, sometimes detailing the fate of its characters." While this book clearly does not merit the label "literary work," this epilogue does try to provide at least a partial answer to the question, "What is next in corporate governance?"

Specifically, we look at three sets of forces that are likely to shape corporate governance systems, principles, and practices in the years to come. We begin with the forces of *globalization*. Societies and corporations are connected by two inter-related sets of laws. The first is the rule of law as defined by local and national legislatures, multilateral agreements, and an emerging body of international law. These legal structures vary greatly from one part of the world to another. Most have deep and ancient societal roots, were shaped through centuries of cultural, political, and economic change, and exhibit a high degree of inertia. Proactive convergence of these structures, therefore, is unlikely, but a new global regulatory framework may be needed.

The market defines the second set of laws. Here we see a very different picture. No matter where a company operates or what it produces, these laws affect, or even determine, its fate. It should not come as a surprise, therefore, that this second set of laws is becoming—within the boundaries of applicable legal structures—the dominant force in the evolution of corporate governance practices around the world.

The second set of forces for change reflects new developments on the *domestic* corporate governance front. As companies continue their struggle to fully comply with the Sarbanes-Oxley Act, new accounting rules and disclosure requirements, and new pressures by institutional investors for greater *shareholder democracy*—principally focused on access and accountability—virtually guarantee further rule changes. The number of shareholder resolutions filed in the most recent proxy season on issues such as majority voting and ballot access has reached an all-time high. Proactive intervention by lawmakers in areas, such as "Say on Pay," is also not out of the question. At the same time, while the trend toward *private equity*-dominated transactions appears to have been dealt a setback by the subprime and leveraged loan financial crisis, the large, privately owned corporation that uses public and private debt rather than public equity as its principal source of capital is likely to be a permanent feature of the global corporate governance landscape.

For the final set of forces, we return to the opening paragraph of the book, which introduced corporate governance in the context of the historical tension between individual freedom and institutional power. As noted in chapter 9, the forces behind the Corporate Social Responsibility (CSR) movement have changed the governance landscape; they effectively have widened the range of players deemed to have a legitimate role in shaping corporate decision making and controlling the exercise of corporate power. Faced with this challenge, the appropriate response by boards is to develop a fuller appreciation of the new governance environment that is emerging. We describe this new environment in terms of a *new compact between business and society.* A key feature of this environment is the increasing pressure on corporations to involve stakeholders in the corporate governance system and holding the corporation answerable to the social claims and demands for nonfinancial information made by stakeholders, just as it is answerable to the financial claims and demands for information made by shareholders.

The Global Convergence of Corporate Governance Practices[1]

The introduction of corporate governance regulations and best practices in one country or region increasingly affects corporate governance practices elsewhere in the world. For example, in 2002 the United Kingdom became the first country to require companies to submit executive compensation proposals to a shareholder vote.[2] Though nonbinding, the votes enable shareholders to voice their concerns on corporate compensation packages. A year later, the Netherlands took the same practice one step further by requiring companies to submit compensation reports to a binding vote by shareholders.[3] If shareholders vote the report down, the company must either keep the previous compensation plan or else call an Extraordinary General Meeting of shareholders for a new vote. In 2005, Sweden and Australia both adopted requirements for nonbinding shareholder votes on compensation.[4] As noted earlier, in the United States, new SEC rules mandate disclosure of executive compensation plans. In addition, a number of recent shareholder resolutions seek an advisory vote on compensation committee reports.

The U.S. Sarbanes-Oxley, along with the implementing requirements that followed, is another example of a standard whose impact extends well beyond national borders. Investors throughout the world have taken notice of Sarbanes-Oxley, and their responses, positive or negative, are shaping the development of regulations and standards in their own countries.

In Japan, perhaps more than anywhere else, the global pressures for governance reform are being felt. And, while change is slow, progress has been made toward providing greater accountability and transparency, a key concern of international investors.

Increasingly, investors use the power of the ballot box to shape corporate governance standards overseas. The 2006 Institutional Shareholder Services (ISS) Global Institutional Investor Study shows that investors in the United States, Canada, and the United Kingdom are the most likely to cast proxy votes outside their home markets, with 73% of U.S., 67% of Canadian, and 60% of U.K. investors voting at least 50% of the shares they hold outside of their home market.[5]

The globalization of corporate governance is also influenced by regulators and governments, especially in developing markets. Markets compete with each other to attract global capital, and that competition includes corporate governance standards. Increasingly, high–corporate governance standards are viewed as a way to make their markets more attractive to international investors.

Global Investor Concerns

The 2006 ISS Global Institutional Investor Study identified three governance issues that consistently rank among the top three concerns of international investors:[6]

- *Better boards*—the independence of the full board and key committees, the process of nominating and electing directors to ensure independence and the right mix of skills and qualifications, the accountability of boards, and their responsiveness to shareholders—defined the number one issue in all markets except Japan. Investors in four markets ranked board structure, composition, or independence as their number one priority, and investors in all markets except the United States included it in their top three issues.
- *Executive pay*—linking pay to performance, disclosing performance metrics, and demonstrating the links justifying executive compensation—was judged critical in all markets but Japan. Some of the strongest concerns came from investors in the United States and Canada.
- *Financial reporting* was a key issue in every market but Australia–New Zealand. More than 70% of investors surveyed cited improved disclosure as the most needed improvement. The lack of trust in current financial reporting extended across markets with distinctive approaches to financial disclosure. U.S. Generally Accepted Accounting Principles (GAAP) came under criticism for its rule-based, sometimes inconsistent or less than informative approach to accounting. The concern over financial reporting was hardly confined to the United States, however. Investors in other markets also voiced concerns, including those that take more of a principles-based approach. In developed markets, the principal challenge was seen to "make sense of the numbers, to see the forest for the trees." In contrast, in developing markets like China, investors worried about obtaining reliable numbers in the first place.

A major conclusion of the survey was that institutional investors increasingly view corporate governance as a business imperative reflecting the recognition that their own business performance is largely driven by the bottom-line performance of the companies in their portfolios. They also signaled that corporate governance is likely to become an even more important factor in investment decisions in the future because of advances in the investment process, including global commercial databases on corporate governance ratings and the proxy voting records of institutional investors.

Global Convergence of Systems, Requirements, and Practices

In 1999 the Organization for Economic Cooperation and Development (OECD) adopted the first multilateral set of guidelines. These "OECD principles" provide a conceptual framework for policymakers, companies, investors, and others to address corporate governance issues in terms that are commonly understood around the world.

The OECD principles define basic requirements a country must meet to be regarded as having an adequate corporate governance environment; they do not target harmonization, per se. Negotiated by lawmakers from 30 major developed economies with widely differing governance standards, they leave considerable room for country differences. They do insist all differences be made transparent, and thereby are a force for convergence. Since their adoption in 1999, the OECD principles have been explicitly used as a benchmark by a number of investor-related initiatives to set guidelines: the International Corporate Governance Network (ICGN)[7] guidelines on corporate governance; the guidelines of some of the largest institutional investors, such as the California Public Employees' Retirement System (CALPERS) and the Teachers' Insurance and Annuity Association–College Retirement Equities Fund (TIAA-CREF) in the United States; and Hermes Asset Management in the United Kingdom. In 2001 the International Institute of Finance (IIF), a grouping of the world's most prominent financial institutions, also issued a set of global guidelines.

Convergence also does not imply a simple victory of one governance system over all others. Corporate ownership and control arrangements are deeply embedded in national laws and culture, and therefore will likely remain at least partly idiosyncratic. Rather, the focus of global alignment is on providing investors with a good understanding of how a company is governed in a particular country and the ability to fairly assess its performance and prospects. In other words, efforts to globally align governance systems and practices view the purpose of a high-quality corporate governance system in terms of generating trust in the investment community.

Convergence is principally occurring in three areas.

The first area concerns *regulations, listing requirements, governance codes, and best practices.* U.S. legislative changes have brought the American regulatory system closer to European norms, including

- the requirement that senior corporate officers must certify the fairness of corporate accounts or face criminal charges;
- the exposure of corporate executives and directors to criminal sanctions if they are found to have defrauded shareholders (the scope of criminal provisions on abuse of corporate property is broader in many continental jurisdictions, especially in France);
- a prohibition on company lending to senior executives (which is illegal in Germany).

Global convergence is also apparent in the new rule by the major U.S. exchanges requiring listed U.S. companies to adopt an internal corporate governance code and a code of ethics. Importantly, while the NYSE is not imposing its listing requirements on listed non-U.S. corporations, it does require them to explicitly comply or explain why they do not comply. This is another important way to stimulate convergence since many of the largest non-U.S. corporations in the world either have or aspire to have a NYSE listing. The new NYSE rules join a growing number of other "comply or explain" codes that have been adopted as part of listing requirements. This middle-of-the road approach between hard mandatory norms and purely voluntary market best practice was pioneered by the London Stock Exchange (LSE) when it integrated the various voluntary codes into a combined code that became a part of its listing requirements.

The second area concerns *board independence and structure, the role and definition of independent directors,* and *shareholder representation.* Board independence is also rapidly becoming a global benchmark. The new U.S. rules have set the independence bar high by requiring that a majority of directors be independent; that the audit, nominating, and compensation committees be comprised exclusively of independent directors and by tightening the definition of independence. But the main thrust of almost every code, whether international or national, is to enhance the independence of the board with regard to the controlling interests in a corporation: the managers in a widely held company or the controlling shareholder, where there is one. Almost all codes address this issue by requiring a "significant" number of independent, nonexecutive directors on the board. Most European codes do not specify a number; Korean listing requirements require that one fourth of the board should be independent; Malaysian listing requirements and the 2001 voluntary Singapore Code put the threshold at one third, following the example of the Vienot Code in France. According to the IIF guidelines, best practice consists in appointing independent directors to fill at least half of the board's seats.

Convergence can also be observed in the opposite direction. Japan, for example, amended its commercial code in May 2002 to allow companies to choose their structure of governance. The choice is between the old company law scheme of a board of directors and a separate audit board, and a new, more U.S.-like structure that provides for an audit committee of the board with independent directors as a majority. Change will be slow; Japanese companies have shied away from instituting a clear board committee structure that would give real responsibilities to a largely ceremonial board.

In Europe, Deutsche Bank made a landmark change in the way its management board is organized, moving away from a focus on collective responsibility to a system that emphasizes individual responsibility of senior officers and the CEO, like that found in the United States. Siemens recently decided to establish an audit committee on its supervisory board (albeit not wholly independent) and to review its own corporate governance annually.

The third area concerns *accounting, disclosure standards,* and *the regulation of the audit function.* The convergence of financial reporting and accounting standards around the world is improving the ability of investors to compare investments on a global basis. It also facilitates accounting and reporting for companies with global operations and eliminates some costly requirements. Still substantially incomplete, it has the potential to create a new standard of accountability and greater transparency.

The goal is an improved reporting model built on principle-based standards. In Phase I of the convergence process (from 2001 to 2005), the European Commission decided on the use of a common financial reporting language (the International Financial Reporting Standards [IFRS]) and required the adoption of IFRS by more than 8,000 companies worldwide. Inaugurated by the February 2006 Memorandum of Understanding between the International Accounting Standards Board (IASB) and the U.S. Financial Accounting Standards Board (FASB), Phase II (from 2006 to 2009) is reserved for rigorous market and regulatory testing of the IFRS and for generating further proposals aimed at addressing significant differences. The objective is the substantial equivalence of IFRS and U.S. GAAP and the elimination of the SEC's reconciliation requirement for foreign private issuers. Looking into the future (Phases III and beyond), the separate standard setters are expected to coordinate their actions and issue substantially identical standards. Longer term elements of FASB could be merged into the IASB structure to create a single, global standard setter (IASB) and accounting framework (IFRS) used worldwide.[8]

Thus, global convergence does not simply imply a movement to globally uniform corporate governance norms and behaviors. Rather, it signals the adoption of principles and practices that allow investors and corporations to increasingly operate on a basis of trust across national borders. Corporations around the world also are beginning to value good corporate governance and are adopting global best practices. In the end, however, the primary force behind global convergence will be investors' demands for better governance and their willingness to value it.

Prospects for Further U.S. Governance Reform

Greater *director independence* to enhance accountability continues to be a major, if not the primary, focus of U.S. governance reform. A quick glance at the list of shareholder proposals of the most recent proxy season confirms this trend. The most popular shareholder resolutions filed concern issues, such as majority voting; access to the proxy statement; declassifying boards; "entrenchment" devices, such as classified boards, poison pills, supermajority vote requirements, and the right to call special shareholder meetings; and, of course, compensation alignment and disclosure. The latter issue, which Monks once called the "smoking gun" of U.S. corporate governance failure, is not only being targeted by shareholders but also by lawmakers.[9]

Majority Voting

During the past year, many institutional shareholders have called on companies to adopt majority voting for director elections as opposed to what has been more common, plurality voting. Under the plurality model, directors who receive the greatest number of favorable votes are elected. Shareholders cannot vote against director nominees but can only withhold or not cast their votes. Thus, most nominees are elected, even if they receive very few favorable votes and even if many votes are withheld or not cast. Under majority voting, to be elected, a nominee must get a majority of the votes cast. The states in which most U.S. public companies are incorporated make either of these models available to corporations.

Companies faced with a majority voting proposal, binding or nonbinding, should pause before adopting the traditional approach of trying to defeat this kind of shareholder proposal. Clearly, investor, and increasingly regulatory, sentiment favors this proposal, and any victory is likely to be short-lived as the proposal will almost certainly be reintroduced every year until it prevails. Moreover, fighting the proposal will be a negative in the company's "corporate governance rating" and may well lead to a new or reinvigorated campaign to withhold votes. Instead, boards would be wise to seize the corporate governance "high ground" by either adopting a modified plurality voting policy or a full-fledged majority voting regime.

Access Proposals

Another corporate governance issue that remains high on activists' lists concerns shareholder proxy access in director elections. A few years ago, the SEC proposed rules that would have allowed certain shareholders to place the names of director nominees in the company's proxy solicitation materials and proxy card. However, after reviewing the proposal, it decided against enactment. Arguments against proxy access included that, under current law, shareholders are free to utilize the proxy rules to solicit votes for their own nominees in director elections. Another argument was that proxy access might allow special interest groups to unduly influence the election process. Not all shareholders have the same interests. Arguments in favor of proxy access were that it would diversify boards and give shareholders a more prominent voice in decision making.

Elimination of "Entrenchment" Devices

Shareholders also continue to fight for the elimination of so-called classified or staggered boards, and the elimination of poison pills and related entrenchment devices. A staggered board of directors occurs when a corporation elects its directors a few at a time, with different groups of directors having overlapping multiyear terms, instead of en masse, with all directors having one-year terms. Each group of directors is put in a specified "class," for example, Class I, Class II, and so on, hence staggered boards are also known as "classified boards." In publicly held companies, staggered boards have the effect of making hostile takeover attempts more difficult because hostile bidders must win more than one proxy fight at successive shareholder meetings in order to exercise control of the target firm. Particularly in combination with a poison pill, a staggered board that cannot be dismantled or evaded is one of the most potent takeover defenses available to U.S. companies. Favole, in the *Wall Street Journal*, reported in January of 2007 that 2006 marked a key switch in the trend toward declassification or annual votes on all directors: More than half

(55%) of the S&P 500 companies have declassified boards, compared with 47% in 2005.[10]

Compensation-Related Proposals

The 2008 proxy season "hot-button" issue was CEO pay, as evidenced by the large number of shareholder proposals calling for an annual advisory shareholder vote on executive pay, so-called "Say on Pay" proposals. Say on Pay is politically and emotionally appealing, attracts positive press, and, most important, is strongly supported by ISS (currently a part of RiskMetrics Group) and other proxy advisory firms. As with the issue of majority voting, given the strong national trend in favor of corporate governance activism and the obvious popular appeal of "Say on Pay," momentum is building toward a pervasive "Say on Pay" regime for U.S. public companies.

The strong momentum for "Say on Pay" is, in part, explained by its international roots. As noted earlier, the concept originated in the United Kingdom in the early 2000s and was made mandatory for LSE-listed companies by an amendment to the Companies Act in 2002. Mandatory shareholder advisory votes on executive compensation have since been legislatively adopted in Australia and Sweden. "Say on Pay" has also been implemented in the Netherlands and Norway in the form of a binding annual "vote of confidence" on executive compensation.

As a practical matter, for a U.S. company, "Say on Pay" means that its executive pay policies and procedures will have to meet ISS guidelines on executive compensation or suffer a very strong risk of ISS recommending that shareholders vote "No on Pay." Such a negative vote, if not addressed promptly by modifying executive compensation to fit ISS guidelines, will almost certainly lead to an ISS withhold-vote recommendation against the compensation committee and perhaps the entire board. The only clearly visible alternative to accepting ISS guidelines on executive compensation is for the board to negotiate exceptions with ISS based on particular facts and circumstances or with investors voting enough shares to overcome an ISS recommendation to vote "No on Pay."

Looking ahead, there are indications that shareholders activists are shifting their focus to shareholder proposals for bylaw amendments to implement corporate governance reform in place of traditional nonbinding shareholder proposals that merely recommend board action. Two major reasons for this change in focus are the continued frustration with company boards that either fail to act in response to a successful nonbinding shareholder resolution or "water down" implementation of the proposal and a concern that boards can too easily amend or rescind board adopted policies under the umbrella of fiduciary duty obligations.

The continued focus of shareholder activists on director independence, director nomination and election, and issues of disclosure and transparency described above is useful and undoubtedly has substantively contributed to improving the U.S. governance system. At the same time, we should ask why they have not adopted a broader and even somewhat bolder agenda for change, especially since it now has been clearly established that increased director independence is not a panacea that will prevent future misconduct—or even managerial inefficiency. Moreover, the evidence in support of a positive relationship between independence and performance is also weak.

As Hinsey (2006) suggests, there *are* corporate governance issues that warrant greater activists' attention. Separating the CEO and chairman positions is chief among them. In most U.S. boardrooms, the CEO continues to serve as board chair. As noted earlier, in this scenario the boardroom leadership responsible for independent directors' oversight of management is the responsibility of none other than the corporation's number one manager, a conflict of interest that is awkward at best.

The obvious solution is separating the two positions—the subject of only a handful of shareholder proposals filed in the last few years. The reason most often given against this idea is that having two leaders is confusing and does not work. The simple fact is, however, that it does work well, as demonstrated by the evidence from Great Britain. And rather than making the recently retired CEO the chairman of the board, outside directors should show their independence by filling the separate chair position with a nonexecutive boardroom leader of their own choosing.[11]

Another potentially productive debate concerns the issue of whether boards and shareholders should talk to each other. Most U.S. companies meet only (infrequently) with their largest shareowners and then only when threatened with resolutions or proxy contests. Resistance to increased communication between directors and investors is typically attributed to current SEC rules. It seems time, however, to test whether these regulations enhance or inhibit stronger corporate governance.

A New Compact Between Business and Society?[12]

A third major force that has already begun to change decision making in boardrooms all around the world is the push for social responsiveness and stakeholder relations. Societal considerations increasingly force companies to rethink their approach to core strategy and business model design. Dealing more effectively with a company's full range of stakeholders is also emerging as a strategic imperative.[1] Historically, the amount of attention paid to stakeholders, other than directly affected parties, such as employees or major investors in crafting strategy, has been limited. Issues pertaining to communities, the environment, the health and happiness of employees, the human rights violations of global supply chains, and activist nongovernmental organizations (NGOs), among numerous other issues, were dealt with by the company's public relations department or its lawyers.

For example, according to Ceres, a coalition of investors and environmental groups that helps coordinate shareholder filings, investors filed a record 43 climate-related resolutions with U.S. companies during the 2007 proxy season.[2] The resolutions sought greater disclosure from companies about their responses to the climate change issue, or called for companies to set greenhouse gas (GHG) reduction targets, and were filed by state and city pension funds and labor, foundation, religious, and other institutional shareholders, managing a total of more than $200 billion in assets.

Fifteen of these resolutions led to positive actions by businesses, leading to shareholders withdrawing their resolutions. Among the companies that addressed investor concerns, oil company ConocoPhillips responded to its resolution by announcing its support for an aggressive mandatory federal policy to reduce GHG emissions, committing to spend $300 million on low-carbon research, including alternative fuels, and agreeing to set a GHG reduction target.

Financial services company Wells Fargo committed to completing GHG assessments of key lending portfolios including agriculture, primary energy production, and power generation, while investment and insurance companies Hartford Insurance and Prudential Financial agreed to improve their public reporting and disclosure regarding the potential risks they face from climate change and strategies for mitigating those risks.

Seven resolutions were filed requesting that companies, including ExxonMobil, set specific GHG reduction targets from their operations and products. These resolutions received strong support, with more that 30% support at ExxonMobil, after investors raised concerns that the company is far behind competitors in addressing climate risks and investing in renewable energy. The increasing support for such resolutions shows that investors are looking for greater transparency about climate risks and information about how companies are preparing to meet the related challenges and seize the opportunities.

In this emerging environment, companies are finding that "business as usual" is no longer an option and that traditional strategies for companies to grow, cut costs, innovate, differentiate, and globalize are now subject to increased scrutiny by all stakeholders. Companies that accept, understand, and embrace this new reality will find that being a "good citizen" has significant, strategic value and does not detract but enhances business success. The late Milton Friedman might have had trouble accepting this new reality, but "good citizenship" has become "the business of business."

APPENDIX A

Sarbanes-Oxley and Other Recent U.S. Governance Reforms

Overview

The Sarbanes-Oxley Act of 2002 imposes significant new disclosure and corporate governance requirements for public companies and also provides for substantially increased liability under the federal securities laws for public companies and their executives and directors. After it was adopted, the NYSE, NASDAQ, and AMEX adopted more comprehensive reporting requirements for listed companies, and the Securities and Exchange Commission (SEC) issued a host of new regulations aimed a strengthening transparency and accountability through more timely and accurate disclosure of information about corporate performance.

The most important changes concern director independence, the composition and responsibilities of the audit, nominating and compensation committees, shareholder approval of equity compensation plans, codes of ethics or conduct, the certification of financial statements by executives, payments to directors and officers of the corporation, the creation of an independent accounting oversight board, and the disclosure of internal controls.

Director Independence

New stock exchange listing requirements stipulate that the majority of directors of public companies be "independent."[1] The rules further state, "No director will qualify as independent unless the board affirmatively determines that the director has no material relationship with the listed company" and require companies to disclose determinations of independence in its annual proxy statement or, if the company does not file an annual proxy statement, in the company's annual report on Form 10-K filed with the SEC.

The rationale for increasing independence was that shareholders, by virtue of their inability to directly monitor management behavior, rely on the board of directors to perform critical monitoring activities and that the board's monitoring potential is reduced, or perhaps eliminated, when management itself effectively controls the actions of the board. Additionally, outside directors may lack independence through various affiliations with the company and may be inclined to support management's decisions in hopes of retaining their relationship with the firm. Requiring a board to have a majority of independent directors therefore increases the quality of board oversight and lessens the possibility of damaging conflicts of interest.

Audit Committees

Rule 10A-3 under the Exchange Act directs the stock exchanges and NASDAQ to require listed companies to have an audit committee composed entirely of independent directors. Subsequent stock exchange and SEC amendments further strengthened this provision by requiring the following, among other things:

- Each member of the audit committee is financially literate, as such qualification is interpreted by the board in its business judgment, or will become financially literate within a reasonable period of time after his or her appointment to the audit committee.
- At least one member of the audit committee is a "financial expert," defined as someone who has
  - o an understanding of financial statements and generally accepted accounting principles;
  - o an ability to assess the general application of such principles in connection with the accounting for estimates, accruals, and reserves;

- o experience preparing, auditing, analyzing, or evaluating financial statements;
- o an understanding of internal controls and procedures for financial reporting;
- o an understanding of audit committee functions.
- The audit committee has a charter that addresses the committee's purpose and sets forth the duties and responsibilities of the committee.
- The audit committee obtains and reviews an annual report by the independent auditor regarding the firm's internal quality-control procedures, discusses the audited financial statements with the independent auditor and management, and reports regularly to the board of directors.
- The audit committee is directly responsible for the appointment, compensation, retention, and oversight of the outside auditors. Additionally, the outside auditors must report directly to the audit committee.
- The audit committee has the authority to engage independent counsel and other advisers, as it determines necessary to carry out its duties.
- The audit committee approves, in advance, any audit or nonaudit services provided by the outside auditors.

The reasons behind these reforms are self-evident. Audit committees are in the best position within the company to identify and act in instances where top management may seek to misrepresent reported financial results. An audit committee composed entirely of outside independent directors can provide independent recommendations to the company's board of directors. The responsibilities of the audit committee include review of the internal audit department, review of the annual audit plan, review of the annual reports and the results of the audit, selection and appointment of external auditors, and review of the internal accounting controls and safeguard of corporate assets.

Compensation Committees

New NYSE and SEC rules require that

- listed companies have a compensation committee composed entirely of independent directors;
- the compensation committee has a written charter that addresses, among other things, the committee's purpose and sets forth the duties and responsibilities of the committee;
- the compensation committee produces—on an annual basis—a compensation committee report on executive compensation, to be included in the company's annual proxy statement or annual report on Form 10-K filed with the SEC.

These reforms respond to the unprecedented growth in compensation for top executives and a dramatic increase in the ratio between the compensation of executives and their employees over the last 2 decades. A reasonable and fair compensation system for executives and employees is fundamental to the creation of long-term corporate value. The responsibility of the compensation committee is to evaluate and recommend the compensation of the firm's top executive officers, including the CEO. To fulfill this responsibility objectively, it is necessary that the compensation committee be composed entirely of outside independent directors.

Nominating Committees

New NYSE and SEC rules stipulate that

- a listed company must have a nominating and corporate governance committee composed entirely of independent directors;
- the nominating and corporate governance committee must have a charter that addresses the committee's purpose and sets forth the goals and responsibilities of the committee.

Nominating new board members is one of the board's most important functions. It is the responsibility of the nominating committee to nominate individuals to serve on the company's board of directors. Placing this responsibility in the hands of an independent nominating committee increases the likelihood that chosen individuals will be more willing to act as advocates for the shareholders and other stakeholders and be less beholden to management.

Shareholder Approval for Equity-Compensation Plans

An equity-compensation plan is a plan or other arrangement that provides for the delivery of equity securities (including options) of the listed company to any service provider as compensation for services. Equity-compensation plans can help align shareholder and management interests, and equity-based awards are often very important components of employee compensation. New NYSE and SEC rules require shareholder approval for stock option plans or other equity compensation plans and any material modification of such plans. These rules are subject to a significant number of exemptions, however. Separately, new accounting rules have changed the accounting of stock options.[2]

Codes of Ethics and Conduct

New rules also require that public companies must adopt and disclose a code of business conduct and ethics for directors, officers, and employees; include its code of business conduct and ethics on its Web site; and each annual report filed with the SEC must state that the code of business conduct and ethics is available on the Web site. The code of conduct must comply with the definition of a "code of ethics" set forth in section 406 of Sarbanes-Oxley and provide for an enforcement mechanism that ensures prompt and consistent enforcement of the code, protection for persons reporting questionable behavior, clear and objective standards for compliance, and a fair process by which to determine violations.

Certification of Financial Statements

Sarbanes-Oxley requires the following:

- The principal executive officers and principal financial officers of public companies should provide a written statement with each periodic report that contains financial statements certifying (a) the report complies with the requirements of section 13(a) or 15(d) of the Exchange Act; and (b) the information contained in the report fairly presents, in all material respects, the financial condition and results of operations of the company

- The above certifications need to be filed separately with the SEC as exhibits to the periodic reports to which they relate.
- The principal executive officer and principal financial officer of the company must certify in each annual and quarterly report that
    - o the certifying officers have reviewed the report;
    - o to the certifying officers' knowledge, the report does not contain any untrue statement of material fact or omit to state a material fact necessary in order to make the statements made, in light of the circumstances under which the statements were made, not misleading;
    - o to the certifying officers' knowledge, the financial statements and other financial information included in the report fairly present, in all material respects, the financial condition and results of operations of the company as of the dates of, and for the periods presented in, the reports;
    - o the certifying officers (a) are responsible for establishing and maintaining effective internal controls, (b) have designed such internal controls to ensure that material information relating to the company is made known to them, (c) have evaluated the effectiveness of the controls as of a date within 90 days prior to the filing of the report, (d) have presented in the report their conclusions about the effectiveness of the controls, (e) have disclosed to their outside auditors and audit committee any significant deficiencies in the internal controls and any fraud involving management or other employees who have a significant role in the company's internal controls, (f) have identified for the outside auditors any material weaknesses in the internal controls, and (g) have indicated in the report whether or not there were significant changes in the internal controls that could affect those controls, including any corrective actions.

Any CEO or CFO who provides the certification knowing that the report does not meet the above-listed standards can be fined up to $1 million, imprisoned for up to 10 years, or both.

Payments to Directors and Officers

Sarbanes-Oxley and subsequent SEC directives stipulate that

- no public company may make a personal loan to a director or officer, and existing loans may not be materially modified or renewed;
- the CEO and CFO of a public company that restates its financial statements as a result of misconduct will have to forfeit any bonuses, incentives, equity-based compensation, and profits on sales of company stock realized during the 12-month period following the first public issuance of the financial document or report containing the inaccurate financial statements;
- the SEC has the authority to freeze any extraordinary payments by the company to any of its directors or officers while an investigation is ongoing;
- the SEC can bar a person who has violated section 17(a) of the Securities Act of 1933 or section 10(b) of the Exchange Act from serving as a public company director or officer;
- directors, officers, and 10% of stockholders of public companies are required to report changes in beneficial ownership within 2 business days after the relevant transaction;
- directors and executive officers are prohibited from buying or selling equity securities during a blackout period;
- nonmanagement directors are required to meet in regularly scheduled executive sessions without management present.

Creation of the PCAOB

The Public Company Accounting Oversight Board (PCAOB) is a private-sector, nonprofit corporation created by Sarbanes-Oxley to oversee accounting professionals who provide independent audit reports for publicly traded companies. Its responsibilities include

- registering public accounting firms;
- establishing auditing, quality control, ethics, independence, and other standards relating to public company audits;
- conducting inspections, investigations, and disciplinary proceedings of registered accounting firms;
- enforcing compliance with Sarbanes-Oxley.

When Congress created the PCAOB, it gave the SEC the authority to oversee the PCAOB's operations, to appoint or remove members, to approve the PCAOB's budget and rules, and to entertain appeals of PCAOB inspection reports and disciplinary actions.

Disclosure of Internal Controls

As directed by section 404 of Sarbanes-Oxley, the SEC adopted a rule requiring registered companies to include in their annual reports a report of management on the company's internal control over financial reporting. The internal control report must include

- a statement of management's responsibility for establishing and maintaining adequate internal controls;
- a management assessment of the effectiveness of the company's internal controls including disclosure of any material weaknesses;
- a statement identifying the framework used by management to evaluate the effectiveness of internal controls;
- a statement that the independent auditors have issued an attestation report on management's assessment of the company's internal controls over financial reporting. In addition, companies must provide disclosure about off-balance-sheet transactions in registration statements, annual reports, and proxy statements.

APPENDIX B

Red Flags in Management Culture, Strategies, and Practices

Analysis of corporations that have experienced major ethical and financial difficulties shows these companies have a great deal in common in terms of their corporate culture and management profiles, as well as their accounting and governance practices. On the basis of this knowledge, we can identify a number of early warning signals, or red flags, boards can use to spot the emergence of a corporate environment and culture susceptible to conflicts of interest and management abuse.

Individually, these factors may not be predictive of future problems. In groups, however, they define a heightened risk profile and should be cause for additional scrutiny and objective analysis. For example, the combination of aggressive management practices creating rapid short-term revenue and stock price growth, coupled with weak board oversight, allowing the CEO to rapidly accumulate personal wealth through stock-based incentive compensation, has been present in a significant percentage of recent problem situations. Risk of rapid financial deterioration in such cases is exacerbated when the company also operates with aggressive financial practices and high leverage.

Specifically, audit committees would be well advised to monitor the following categories of higher risk characteristics based on their proven usefulness in identifying corporate environments that may be susceptible to rapid stock price and credit deterioration, as well as fraud:

This appendix is from Wood (2005).

- *Business Growth Strategy and Record*
  - o Aggressive pursuit of growth through acquisitions or through rapid expansion into new business lines, industries, or markets
  - o Major or frequent shifts or U-turns in business or operational strategy, including history of restructuring or sale of core business units or assets
  - o History of setting business growth targets, strategies, and projections that appear aggressive or overly optimistic, especially in comparison to peers
  - o Growth materially in excess of peers or broader market
- *Equity Culture: Stock Price Appreciation Strategy and Management Ownership*
  - o Aggressive positioning as a "growth stock"
  - o Overpreoccupation of management on short-term stock-price appreciation
  - o Low or no common dividend policy
  - o Rapid accumulation of ownership (stock and options) by senior management, at a rate and to levels materially in excess of peer group
  - o Long-established CEO and senior management team with significant ownership interest where structural complexity, leverage, or opaqueness are present
  - o Growth in price–earnings ratio, stock price, or market capitalization materially in excess of peers
- *Senior Management Character, Compensation, Composition, Tenure, Turnover, and Succession*
  - o Cult of a CEO (leader) personality or the high media profile of CEO
  - o Over-reliance on, excessive power of, or domination by the CEO, including unwillingness to delegate
  - o Heavy dependence on the CEO for corporate public, client, and government relations (e.g., when the CEO is the sole or main spokesperson)
  - o Weak or "domineered" senior management team below the CEO
  - o CEO incentive and/or total compensation materially higher than peer average

- o Link between company financial performance and executive compensation primarily focused on short-term horizon
- o Special payments or unusual fringe benefits or loans to executives without a clear purpose, or unconnected with any increase in performance (including "guaranteed" bonuses)
- o Compensation plans or provisions that create perverse incentives (i.e., payouts that encourage excessive acquisition activity; payouts on reaching a certain share price trading level).
- o Unclear succession plan and/or failure to name a successor
- o High or unexpected senior management or board of director turnover or departures.
- o Lack of credibility in company explanation of senior departure(s)
- o Lavish CEO and senior executive lifestyle and corporate entertainment

- *Corporate Culture and Business Practices*
  - o Lack of meaningful long-term corporate planning and focus
  - o Creation of a "culture of greed" and management self-enrichment: materially more generous compensation pattern for the CEO and senior executives than peers
  - o "Make the numbers!" corporate culture: untoward pressure on managers to achieve aggressive budgets
  - o Creation of a "culture of fear," penalizing internal debate and independent or creative thinking; creation of environment where only "good news" is acceptable to corporate chieftains
  - o "Take no prisoners!" corporate culture: questionable or heavy-handed strategies and tactics with competitors, customers, employees, suppliers, accountants, bankers, business partners, and regulators or government authorities
  - o History of litigation in pursuit of business strategies and undue pressure on critics (e.g., lawsuits by company against company customers, employees, suppliers, accountants, bankers, regulators or government entities)
  - o Lack of transparency: history of lack of openness with external and internal constituencies, including independent directors
  - o Heavy use of lobbyists and lawyers

  o Aggressive corporate communication and image building; heavy
     use of "spin"
  o History of aggressive or questionable sales and/or marketing
     practices
  o Cavalier attitudes toward internal control
- *Company's Legal, Business, Financial, Ownership, and Tax
  Practices*
  o Major changes in ownership, managerial, legal, regulatory, and
     operating structure
  o Overfocus of management time and resources on creating com-
     plex corporate legal entity, operating, finance, and tax structures
     (particularly if this is accompanied by intercompany asset sales,
     transfers, or fee payments)
  o Existence of seemingly excessive number of corporate legal entity
     vehicles (particularly those with limited or no clear operational
     mandates)
  o Heavy reliance on tax shelters or similar devices to maintain or
     maximize profitability
  o Management inability or unwillingness to explain reasons behind
     corporate-, finance-, tax-, or ownership-structure complexities
  o Aggressiveness or complexity in financial leverage and structure,
     including
     - high degree of leverage versus peers;
     - stability of capital structure susceptible to refinancing risk;
     - over-reliance on short-term debt;
     - management inability to explain rationale for capitalization
        structure and financing sources and uses;
     - complexity or untoward number of financing subsidiaries or
        other financing vehicles within the corporate structure;
     - Overly structured financing arrangements.
  o Financial stability and liquidity sensitive to triggers, contingents,
     or access to nonoperating sources of cash, including
     - existence of material triggers in debt, derivative and operating
        agreements calling for repayment or collateralization of debt
        or contingents given certain predefined events;
     - lack of credible contingency funding plan;

- over-reliance on receivables sales and factoring;
- danger of tripping covenant thresholds;
- access or ability to borrow curtailed, increased cost of borrowing;
- financial viability (debt service or access to capital) dependent on assets sales, extraordinary contingent realizations, or unusually large cash reserves (at borrower or subsidiaries).

- *Accounting, Disclosure Practices, and Reported Results*
  - o Aggressive strategy or history of revenue or income recognition and understating costs or liabilities, including
    - net income growth materially higher than recurring cash flow growth;
    - revenue, income growth, or both, materially higher than peers;
    - aggressive use of "pro-forma" adjustments;
    - litigation or regulatory action charging illicit financial reporting practices;
    - history of understating costs or liabilities or overstating revenue;
    - history of restatements, accounting errors and irregularities, and nonrecurring and special charges;
    - large percentage of revenues and net income from nonoperating, nonrecurring sources, or both;
    - Use of aggressive accounting elections or assumptions.
  - o Aggressiveness, problems, frequent changes, and complexity in accounting practices and reporting, including
    - frequent changes in accounting elections and treatments, especially those affecting revenue, cost, and liability reporting;
    - history of changes in, or disputes with, auditors;
    - auditor providing qualified opinion or refusal to sign financials;
    - history of late filing or issuance of financials;
    - weak internal control environment;
    - nontransparent or lacking financial disclosure;
    - weak internal audit function, ineffective audit committee, or both;

- external constituents' difficulty in understanding reported results or financials because of complexity in operational structure or lack of comparability between reporting periods (e.g., due to impact of successive acquisitions or dispositions), or both.

- *Litigation, Regulatory, and Governmental Actions and Track Record*
  o High or increasing incidence in litigation, or threat thereof, from customers, vendors, competitors, regulators, shareholders, creditors, or government entities
  o Lawsuits suggesting the development of overly aggressive or illicit corporate culture in areas including management misrepresentations, product deficiency, excessive executive compensation and benefits or perks, company loans to executives, accounting and reporting irregularities, fraudulent or coercive sales, price fixing and illegal "market cornering" activities, or failure to supervise (management negligence)
  o Sizable contingent liabilities exist or have material chance of developing; establishment of material reserves for future litigation costs/liabilities
  o Increased incidence of regulatory scrutiny, actions, or penalties (including forced restatement, refiling of various reports or tax audits)

APPENDIX C

Enterprise Risk Management

Questions for the Board

The recent wave of business scandals and threatening world events has fostered a greater awareness of the importance of risk management as a component of corporate governance. In 2004, the so-called Committee of Sponsoring Organizations of the Treadway Commission (COSO) released a comprehensive report titled "Enterprise Risk Management—Integrated Framework" to provide companies with a roadmap for identifying risks, avoiding pitfalls, and taking advantage of opportunities to grow firm value.

COSO defines enterprise risk management (ERM) as

> a process, effected by an entity's board of directors, management and other personnel, applied in a strategy setting and across the enterprise, designed to identify potential events that may affect the entity, and manage risk to be within its risk appetite, to provide reasonable assurance regarding the achievement of entity objectives.[1]

So defined, ERM assists in

- *aligning risk appetite and strategy* by explicitly considering the organization's risk appetite in evaluating strategic alternatives, setting related objectives, and developing mechanisms to manage related risks;

This appendix is from Waller, Lansden, Dortch, and Davis (2005).

- *enhancing risk response decisions* by providing rigor to identifying and selecting among alternative risk responses—risk avoidance, reduction, sharing, and acceptance;
- *reducing operational surprises and losses* by enhancing the capability to identify potential events and establish responses, thereby reducing surprises and associated costs or losses;
- *identifying and managing multiple and cross-enterprise risks* by facilitating integrated responses to multiple risks across the organization;
- *seizing opportunities* by considering a full range of potential events, which allows management to identify and proactively realize opportunities;
- *improving deployment of capital* by obtaining robust risk information, which allows management to effectively assess overall capital needs and enhance capital allocation.

Whereas traditional risk-management approaches are focused on protecting tangible assets shown on a company's balance sheet and related contractual rights and obligations, the scope and application of ERM are much broader. ERM's focus is *enterprise-wide*, and on *enhancing as well as protecting the tangible and intangible assets* that define a company's business model. This widening of the scope of risk management reflects the fact that—with market capitalizations often significantly higher than historical balance-sheet values—the extension of risk management to intangible assets is critical. Just as future events can affect the value of tangible physical and financial assets, they can also affect the value of key intangible assets, such as a company's reputation with suppliers, innovation record, or its brands.

ERM explicitly recognizes that risk may originate inside or outside the organization. For example, *environmental* risk originates outside the organization and can impair the viability of a particular business model. *Process* risk factors tend to be internal in origin and affect the ability of the firm to execute its stated mission. *Information for decision-making* risk threatens value creation because of its impact on the timeliness, quality, reliability, and comprehensiveness the information used to make key decisions.

Because risks do not always fall clearly into one category, the ERM philosophy encourages companies to develop a comprehensive risk-management plan in which the approaches to the various components of risk interact with and influence one another. In particular, ERM looks at eight sets of issues:

- *Internal environment.* The tone of an organization is set at the top of the organization. It is, therefore, important to ask what appetite its leaders have for risk and whether the company's culture supports the chosen risk profile and risk-management and internal controls process.
- *Objective setting.* Companies typically set goals on many levels: strategic, operating, and financial. By clearly identifying its goals, management and the board can more clearly perceive the risks that the company may encounter.
- *Event identification.* The board should ask management how the company identifies new risks and opportunities. What risks and trends exist in the company's industry? What risks are associated with new products, services, or acquisitions? With new competitors? How are the company's risks interrelated? The board should also consider legal, ethical, and compliance risks that the company may encounter.
- *Risk assessment.* After identifying potential risks, management and the board should analyze and prioritize the risks in light of their likelihood and potential impact. Each business unit should be involved in the process and ask questions, such as, What adverse events has the company encountered in the past, and what lessons were learned?
- *Risk response.* Companies may chose to respond to risks by avoiding them or by accepting them and working to reduce their impact or dilute their severity by sharing risk with other parties. This raises questions, such as, What are the costs of these alternatives? Has management allocated sufficient resources to respond appropriately? Is the company adequately insured for its insurable risks?

- *Control activities.* The board should work with management to develop and implement well-structured policies and procedures in response to the company's primary risks to ensure that responsive actions are carried out at all levels of the company.
- *Information and communication.* Relevant information should be well documented and communicated on a timely basis—vertically, up and down the chain of management, and horizontally, across divisions of a company—to ensure that all members of the organization carry out their responsibilities with respect to the company's risk-management policies.
- *Monitoring.* The board should help management establish testing and evaluation procedures to monitor the company's risk-management system. Modifications to the risk-management system should be made as needed in response to these evaluations.

Although the management of a company is ultimately responsible for a company's risk management, the board must understand the risks facing the company and oversee the risk-management process. Board committees should incorporate risk management into their regular responsibilities. A company's governance committee can ensure that the company is prepared to deal with risks and crises by evaluating the individual capabilities of the directors, nominating directors with crisis-management experience, and considering the time each director and nominee has to devote to the company. The governance committee should also work with management to establish an orientation program for new directors and succession plans for key executive officers.

While some companies prefer to involve the board as a whole in the risk-management process, corporate governance guidelines and charters of audit committees may delegate this responsibility to the audit committee. Alternatively, a company may appoint a risk-management officer, form a risk-management committee, or assign responsibility to a finance or compliance committee of the board. The responsible committee or group should meet regularly with the company's internal auditor, the chief financial officer, the general counsel, and the head of compliance and individual business units to discuss specific risks and assess the effectiveness of the company's risk-management systems.

Board committees should also incorporate risk management into their regular responsibilities. A company's governance committee can ensure that the company is prepared to deal with risks and crises by evaluating the individual capabilities of the directors, nominating directors with crisis management experience, and considering the time each director and nominee has to devote to the company. The governance committee should also work with management to establish an orientation program for new directors and succession plans for key executive officers.

Questions Boards Should Ask About Risk Management

The NYSE listing requirements specify that, when addressing the audit committee's duties and responsibilities, the committee charter should state that the committee must discuss management's policies with respect to risk assessment and management. The ERM framework provides a context for such a discussion. Examples of questions the committee should ask include

- *with respect to strategy,*
  1. Is the board effectively engaged in strategic discussion of the company's appetite for risk taking?
  2. Does management involve the board when making decisions to accept or reject significant risks?
  3. Is the company taking risks the board does not understand?
  4. Are the risks inherent to the company's business model fully understood? Managed capably? Monitored in a timely fashion?
- *with respect to policy,*
  1. How does management reward growth and innovation without creating unacceptable exposure to risk? Are there defined boundaries and limits that clearly specify behaviors that are off-limits?
  2. Is there a proper balance between entrepreneurial and control activities? Are the risks associated with opportunity seeking clearly understood and managed?

- *with respect to execution,*
  1. Does management understand the uncertainties inherent in its strategies for the business?
  2. Are there assurances that risk controls function properly?
  3. Does the company have effective contingency plans to respond in event of a crisis?
  4. What system of "early warning" signals does the company have?
  5. Are there effective processes in place for identifying, measuring, and evaluating risk-management capabilities?
  6. Has a risk officer or risk-management team been appointed?
- *with respect to transparency,*
  1. Is there an effective process for reliable reporting on risks and risk-management performance?
  2. Does the company have an organizational structure in place to support enterprise-wide risk management?

Notes

Introduction

1. Centre of European Policy Studies (CEPS; 1995), as reported in Shleifer and Vishny (1997).

2. European Corporate Governance Institute (1992).

3. Organization for Economic Cooperation and Development (OECD; 1999).

Chapter 1

1. Agency theory explains the relationship between principals, such as shareholders and agents, like a company's executives. In this relationship, the principal delegates or hires an agent to perform work. The theory attempts to deal with two specific problems: first, that the goals of the principal and agent are not in conflict (agency problem) and second, that the principal and agent reconcile different tolerances for risk.

2. This section is based on Kenneth Holland's May 2005 review of the book *Corporate Governance: Law, Theory and Policy.*

3. http://www.sec.gov/about/whatwedo.shtml

4. http://www.investopedia.com

5. This section draws on Edwards (2003).

6. Citigroup paid $400 million to settle government charges that it issued fraudulent research reports; and Merrill Lynch agreed to pay $200 million for issuing fraudulent research in a settlement with securities regulators and also agreed that, in the future, its securities analysts would no longer be paid on the basis of the firm's related investment-banking work.

7. Coffee (2002, 2003a, 2003b).

8. Bradley, Schipani, Sundaram, and Walsh (1999).

9. Bradley, Schipani, Sundaram, and Walsh (1999).

10. Bradley, Schipani, Sundaram, and Walsh (1999).

11. This section is based on the essay by Hawley and Williams (2001).

12. Thornton (2002, January 14). Hostile takeovers made a dramatic comeback after the 2001 to 2002 economic recession. In 2001, the value of hostile takeovers climbed to $94 billion, more than twice the value in 2000 and almost $15 billion more than in 1988, the previous peak year.

13. Romano (1994).

14. Holmstrom and Kaplan (2003).

15. Lindstrom (2008).

16. "MCI, Inc.," Microsoft® Encarta® Online Encyclopedia (2008).

17. Edwards (2003).

Chapter 2

1. Bernstein (December 2007–January 2008).

2. See Bebchuk (2007, May), p. 675; and Lipton and Savitt (2007, May), p. 733.

3. Lipton and Savitt (2007, May), p. 733.

4. See *The American Law Institute* (1994), pp. 61.

5. See, for example, Bradley, Schipani, Sundaram, and Walsh (1999), pp. 9–86; and Matheson and Olson (1992), pp. 1313–1391.

6. *Reason* (2005, October).

7. Friedman (1970).

8. Friedman (1970).

9. Drucker (1974), p. 67.

10. This section draws on Sundaram and Inkpen (2004).

11. *Dodge v. Ford Motor Co.* (1919).

12. Dodd (1932), pp. 1145–1163.

13. Friedman (1970).

14. For agency theory, see, for example, Alchian and Demsetz (1972); and Jensen and Meckling (1976); and Fama and Jensen (1983a). Agency theory is directed at the dilemma in which one party (the shareholder as the principal) delegates work to another (management as the agent) who performs that work. Agency theory is concerned with resolving two problems that can occur in such a relationship. The first is the agency problem that arises when (a) the desires or goals of the principal and agent conflict and (b) it is difficult or expensive for the principal to verify what the agent is actually doing. The issue here is that the principal cannot verify that the agent has behaved appropriately. The second is the problem of risk sharing that arises when the principal and agent have different attitudes toward risk. In this situation, the principle and the agent may prefer different actions because of the different risk preferences.

15. Easterbrook and Fischel (1991). Nexus of contracts theory views the firm not as an entity but as an aggregate of various inputs brought together to produce goods or services. Employees provide labor. Creditors provide debt capital. Shareholders initially provide equity capital and subsequently bear the risk of losses and monitor the performance of management. Management monitors the performance of employees and coordinates the activities of all the firm's inputs. The firm is seen as simply a web of explicit and implicit contracts establishing rights and obligations among the various inputs making up the firm.

16. See the notes for Bainbridge (1993) "In Defense of the Shareholder Wealth Maximization Norm: A Reply to Professor Green."

17. Lorsch (with MacIver) (1989), chap. 3.

18. Lorsch (with MacIver) (1989), p. 49.

19. Carter and Lorsch (2004), p. 57.

20. McTaggart, Kontes, and Mankins (1994), chap. 1.

21. Ellsworth (2002), p. 6.

22. Jensen (2001), pp. 297–317.

23. McTaggart et al. (1994), chap. 1.

24. Freeman (1984), p. 17.

25. Davis (2006, November 1).

26. Henry Schacht, quoted in *Fortune*, July 7, 2003, and referred to in Martin, "The Coming Corporate Revolt" (2003), p. 1.

27. See Jensen and Meckling (1976); Fama (1980), pp. 291–293; and Fama and Jensen (1983b). For a somewhat different view, see Klein (1982).

28. Freeman and McVea (2001), p. 194.

29. Bainbridge (1994).

30. Under the Delaware code, shareholder voting rights are essentially limited to the election of directors and the approval of charter or bylaw amendments, mergers, sales of substantially all of the corporation's assets, and voluntary dissolutions. As a formal matter, only the election of directors and the amendment of the bylaws do not require board approval before shareholder action is possible. See Delaware Code Ann. tit. 8, §§ 109, 211 (1991). In practice, of course, even the election of directors, absent a proxy contest, is predetermined by the existing board nominating the following year's board.

31. As a practical matter, of course, the sheer mechanics of undertaking collective action by thousands of shareholders preclude them from meaningfully affecting management decisions.

32. Jensen (2001), p. 16.

33. Jensen (2001), p. 16.

34. Jensen (2001), p. 17.

Chapter 3

1. See the *Corporate Director's Guidebook* (4th ed., 2004), the American Bar Association.

2. This book focuses on the most important laws aimed at guiding directors' behavior. The reader should be aware that the law includes additional duties for directors such as "the duty not to entrench" and "the duty of supervision."

3. Indemnification of officers and directors means that the corporation will reimburse them for expenses incurred and amounts paid in defending claims brought against them for actions taken on behalf of the corporation. Insurance

policies can cover matters that cannot be indemnified under state law or in instances where the corporation does not have the financial resources to pay for the indemnification. Most state corporation statutes allow corporations to purchase insurance to cover matters resulting from acts taken by officers and directors. The goal of directors and officers insurance is to protect directors and officers of a corporation from liability in the event of a claim or lawsuit against them asserting wrongdoing in connection with the company's business.

4. Business Roundtable (2005), p. 2.

5. Milstein, Holly, and Grapsas (2006, January).

6. Buffett, annual letter to Berkshire Hathaway shareholders (1993).

7. Buffett (1993).

8. Buffett (1993).

9. Jones (2007).

10. See, for example, Felton and Pamela Fritz (2005); and The State of the Corporate Board, 2007—A McKinsey Global Survey (2007, April).

11. Carver (2007, November), pp. 1030–1037.

12. Carver (2007, November), p. 1035.

13. Macavoy and Milstein (2003).

14. The statistics in this chapter are taken from the Spencer Stuart Board Index 2007.

15. Heidrick and Struggles (2006).

16. Macavoy and Milstein (2003), pp. 22–23.

17. Carter and Lorsch (2004), p. 93.

18. This finding is reported in a September 2004 study of more than 2,500 companies across the world by Governance Metrics International, the New York–based corporate governance ratings agency.

19. Coombes and Wong (2004).

20. Coombes and Wong (2004).

Chapter 4

1. For a more detailed summary of these and related governance reforms, see, for example, Morgan Lewis, Counselors at Law, "Corporate Governance: An Overview of Recently Adopted Reforms" (2004); or Petra, "Corporate Governance Reforms: Fact or Fiction, Corporate Governance" (2006), pp. 107–115.

2. Edwards (2003).

3. The term "earnings mismanagement" is used in the widest sense to include not only reporting that is illegal or inconsistent with accepted accounting standards but also statements that, while within accepted legal accounting standards, are primarily meant to deceive investors about the company's true financial condition

4. Hall and Murphy (2002), p. 42.

5. It is now also recognized that a change in tax law—the addition of section 162(m) to the IRS code—was a major contributor to the increased use of stock options. For more on this subject, see chapter 8 in this volume.

6. Edwards (2003).

7. Edwards (2003).

8. See Enron's proxy statement, May 1, 2001. Subsequent to Enron's collapse, the independence of some Enron directors was questioned by the press and in Senate hearings because some directors received consulting fees in addition to board fees. Enron had made donations to groups with which some directors were affiliated and had also done transactions with entities in which some directors played a major role.

9. The beneficial ownership of the outside directors reported in the 2001 proxy ranged from $266,000 to $706 million. See Gillan and Martin (2002), p. 23.

10. See Gordon (2003).

11. This subcommittee is administered by the Permanent Subcommittee on Investigations, Committee on Governmental Affairs, United States Senate, July 8, 2002.

12. Warren Buffett's letter to Berkshire Hathaway shareholders, as quoted in *USA Today*, March 31, 2003.

13. Edwards (2003).

14. As noted by Edwards (2003), Citigroup paid $400 million to settle government charges that it issued fraudulent research reports; and Merrill Lynch agreed to pay $200 million for issuing fraudulent research in a settlement with securities regulators and also agreed that, in the future, its securities analysts would no longer be paid on the basis of the firm's related investment-banking work. Also see Coffee (2002, 2003a, 2003b); Stewart and Countryman (2002).

15. The popular question, "Do you know anyone who washes a rental car?" is appropriate here.

16. The Securities and Exchange Act of 1934 requires that at least 50% of the value of a fund's total assets satisfy two criteria: an equity position cannot exceed 5% of the value of a fund's assets, and the fund cannot hold more then 10% of the outstanding securities of any company.

17. These questions are adapted from Edwards (2003). We also note that the Securities and Exchange Commission (SEC) recently made progress on this issue by requiring that a majority of mutual fund boards be comprised of "independent" directors, and by changing the definition of "independence" to be the same as that employed by Sarbanes-Oxley and the New York Stock Exchange.

18. Berle and Means (1932), p. 62; Mace (1971), p. 3; Drucker (1974), p. 628; and Gillies (1992), p. 3.

19. Lorsch and MacIver (1989).

20. Leighton and Thain (1997), p. 51.

21. Monks (2005, March), p. 108.

22. Monks (2005, March), p. 109.

23. Monks (2005, March), p. 109.

24. Monks (2005, March), p. 110.

25. In academic terms, reforms enacted to date can be characterized as being primarily focused on addressing the so-called agency problem—the innate conflict that exists between owners (investors) and management, even though managers ostensibly act in the shareholders' interests. For more on this issue, see chapter 3.

Chapter 5

1. Mercer Delta (2006), Governance Surveys.

2. Lucier, Kocourek, and Habbel (2006).

3. Khurana, Rakesh, and Cohn (2003, Spring).

4. Felton and Fritz (2005).

5. This section draws on "The board of directors' role in CEO succession," (2006) interview with Heidrick & Struggles, "Building high-performance boards"; and Lucier et al. (2006).

6. This section is based on Lucier et al. (2006) and Charan (2005, February).

7. Charan (2005), p. 75.

8. Charan (2005), p. 76.

9. "The Role of the Board in CEO Succession," a best practices study published by the National Association of Corporate Directors (NACD) in collaboration with Mercer Delta Consulting, April 2006.

Chapter 6

1. Keinath and Walo (2004), p. 23.

2. For an example of an audit committee charter, consult the Web site of any major public corporation.

3. This section is based on The Institute of Internal Auditors (2006), "The Audit Committee—Purpose, Process, Professionalism." http://www.theiia.org

4. Buffett, annual letter to Berkshire Hathaway shareholders (2002).

5. This section is based on Kleinman and Thompson (2002).

6. The leading Delaware cases addressing the duty of oversight and related issues are *Graham v. Allis-Chalmers Mfg. Co.* (1963); *In re Caremark International Derivative Litigation* (1996); *Aronson v. Lewis* (1984); *Boeing Co. v. Shrontz* (1992); and *In re Dataproducts Corp. Shareholders Litigation* (1991). See also Hansen (1993).

7. This section is based on Wood (2005).

8. For a more detailed discussion of this subject, see Waller, Lansden, Dortch, and Davis (2005) and Appendix C.

9. Web site of Berkshire Hathaway, available at http://www.berkshirehathaway .com.

Chapter 7

1. Bart (2004), pp. 111–125.
2. Lorsch (1995, January–February).
3. Felton and Fritz (2005).
4. de Kluyver and Pearce (2009), chap. 1.
5. Bart (2004).
6. Carey and Patsalos-Fox (2006).
7. Korn/Ferry (2007).
8. Nadler (2004).
9. Nadler (2004).
10. Nadler (2004).
11. Nadler (2004).
12. This section is based on de Kluyver and Pearce (2008), chap. 9; and Rérolle and Vermeire (2005, April 29).

13. Usually, such opinions are prepared by the company's financial advisers or other consultants hired by management (who naturally hope to gain repeat business). The board must ensure that this expert appraisal is carried out in a truly independent manner. The board must therefore verify the independence and skills of the expert(s), and, when the report is submitted, it must ensure that the work was carried out properly, in accordance with the professional standards in force. This assumes that at least one member of the board has adequate, relevant experience or that the board is assisted by another expert to help it in this task of supervision.

14. Rérolle and Vermeire (2005, April 29).

15. This section is based on "What directors know about their companies: A McKinsey Survey" (2006, March).

16. This section is based on Nadler (2004).

17. Carey and Patsalos-Fox (2006).

Chapter 8

1. This section is based on Rivero and Nadler (2003).
2. Spencer Stuart Board Index 2007.
3. Rivero and Nadler (2003).
4. Rivero and Nadler (2003).

5. Rivero and Nadler (2003).

6. Rivero and Nadler (2003).

7. Data from The Corporate Library is based on 211 proxy statements filed in 2008 through April 9.

8. Economic Research Institute (ERI) press release, February 15, 2008.

9. *Financial Week*, March 28, 2008. See also Equilar (2008).

10. E-mail from Angelo Mozilo to John England, November 24, 2006, released by the U.S. House Oversight and Government Reform Committee. Mozilo renegotiated his contract with Countrywide for an annual salary of $1.9 million, an incentive bonus of between $4 million and $10 million, perks and fringe benefits, as well as $37.5 million in severance benefits. Under public pressure, he subsequently agreed to give up the severance package.

11. Crystal (1992).

12. McCarroll (1992).

13. *Wall Street Journal*, February 14, 1992.

14. Rose and Wolfram (2002, pp. S138–S175) document a "spike" in base salaries at $1 million that did not exist before the new tax rules.

15. This argument ignores possible inside information held by the employee about the prospects of the firm, and the potential incentive benefits accruing to shareholders when employees hold options.

16. Murphy and Zabojnik (2003).

Chapter 9

1. The SEC regulates and promulgates rules governing shareholder resolutions.

2. Thompson Financial (2007).

3. World Investment Report (2004).

4. The International Chamber of Commerce, a global advocacy group for the private sector, observed in 2000 that "non-governmental organizations have gained an enormous influence" over corporate decision making, as quoted in Barrington (2000, January–June).

5. "Civil society" is sometimes described as the part of society that exists between the state and the market. A more formal definition is "the voluntary association of citizens, promoting their values and interests in the public domain," according to Saxby and Schacter (2003, p. 4). Kaldor, Anheier, and Glasius (2003, p. 2) estimate that there are approximately 48,000 international nongovernmental organizations (NGOs), and that total membership in international NGOs grew by about 70% between 1990 and 2000.

6. "Big investors want SRI research: European institutions to allocate part of brokers' fees to 'nontraditional' information," *Financial Times* (UK), October 18, 2004.

7. This section is based on M. Nadler (2004) and D. Nadler, Behan, and M. Nadler (2006).

8. Bremer (2006).

9. Myers (2007, January–February).

Chapter 10

1. Heidrick and Struggles (2006).

2. Bird, Buchanan, and Rogers (2004).

3. Bird, Buchanan, and Rogers (2004), p. 130.

4. Spencer Stuart (2008).

5. Spencer Stuart (2008).

6. For more on formal versus informal rules in the boardroom, see Carter and Lorsch (2004), chap. 8. See also Khurana and Pick (2005), pp. 1259–1285.

7. Carter and Lorsch (2004), chap. 7.

8. *Directorship* July 11, 2008.

9. Brancato and Plath (2004). Many CEOs have historically followed a practice that all communication of information to the board from senior managers would flow first through the CEO, who would then relay that information to the board. This has the potential to obstruct information flow to the board. See also Ide (2003, March), p. 838.

10. For additional thoughts on this subject, see Anderson (2006).

Chapter 11

1. This section draws on the 2006 Global Institutional Investor Study "Corporate Governance: From Compliance Obligation to Business Imperative," by Institutional Shareholder Services (2006).

2. The "Directors Remuneration Report Regulations" became part of U.K. company law in 2002 and took effect the following year. The government adopted the regulations in response to concerns about excessive pay for poor performance. The new requirement is mandatory for all companies listed on the LSE index—a total of 980 companies as of March 2006. These companies must submit a remuneration report that contains a wide range of information, including cash pay, share and option grants, and performance targets for long-term plans. Companies must put the remuneration report to a nonbinding shareholder vote at the annual general meeting.

3. The Tabaksblat Code of December 2003 requires that proposed remuneration policies be submitted to the general shareholders meeting for approval.

4. This element of the Swedish Code of Corporate Governance took effect on July 1, 2005.

5. ISS (2006), Global Institutional Investor Study (2006).

6. Global Institutional Investor Study (2006), p. 36.

7. The International Corporate Governance Network (ICGN) is an association of large institutional investors from around the world with more than 10 trillion assets, under management whose aim is to promote better governance globally. For more details about the ICGN, go to their Web site, http://www.isgn.org

8. PriceWaterHouseCoopers ViewPoint (2007, April).

9. Monks (2005, March), p. 108.

10. Favole (2007).

11. Hinsey (2006).

12. This section draws heavily on Rochlin (2006).

13. "Pressure grows on U.S. companies to act on climate," *Environmental Finance* magazine, http://www.environmental-finance.com

Appendix A

1. An exception is made for "controlled companies"—those for which more than 50% of the voting power is held by an individual, a group, or other company.

2. For more on this subject, see chapter 8 in this volume.

Appendix C

1. PricewaterhouseCoopers (2004). Principles-Based Framework for Managements and Boards to Comprehensively Manage Risks to Objectives (released by COSO, available at http://www.coso.org).

References

Alchian, A. A., & Demsetz, H. (1972). Production, information costs, and economic organization. *American Economic Review, 62,* 777–795.

American Bar Association. (2004). *Corporate director's guidebook* (4th ed.). Committee on Corporate Laws, ABA Section of Business Law. Chicago: American Bar Association.

American Law Institute. (1994). *Principles of corporate governance: Analysis and recommendations.* Philadelphia: Author.

Bainbridge, S. M. (1993). In defense of the shareholder wealth maximization norm: A reply to Professor Green. *Washington and Lee Law Review, 50,* 1423.

Barrington, L. (2000). Business, government and civil society—Working together for a better world. *Asian Review of Public Administration, 12*(1).

Bart, C. (2004). The governance role of the board in corporate strategy: An initial progress report. *International Journal of Business Governance and Ethics, 1*(2/3), 111–125.

Bebchuk, L. (2007, May). The myth of the shareholder franchise. *Virginia Law Review, 93*(3), 675.

Berle, A. A., Jr., & Means, G. C. (1932). *The modern corporation and private property.* New York: Commerce Clearing House.

Bernstein, A. (December 2007–January 2008). Lipton vs. Bebchuck. *Directorship, 33*(6), 20–25.

Bird, A., Buchanan, R., & Rogers, P. (2004). The seven habits of an effective board. *European Business Journal, 16*(3), 128–132.

Bradley, M., Schipani, C. A., Sundaram, A. K., & Walsh, J. P. (1999). The purposes and accountability of the corporation in contemporary society: Corporate governance at a crossroads. *Law and Contemporary Problems, 62*(3), 9–86.

Brancato, C., & Plath, C. (2004). *Corporate governance best practices: A blueprint for the post-Enron era.* New York: The Conference Board.

Buffett, W. (1993). Annual letter to Berkshire Hathaway shareholders. Available from Berkshire Hathaway Corporation.

Business Roundtable. (2005). *Principles of governance and American competitiveness.* Washington, DC: Author.

Carey, D. C., & Patsalos-Fox, M. (2006). Shaping strategy from the boardroom. *McKinsey Quarterly, 3,* 90–94.

Carter, C. B., & Lorsch, J. W. (2004). *Back to the drawing board—Designing corporate boards for a complex world.* Boston: Harvard Business School Press.

Carver, J. (2007, November). The promise of governance theory: Beyond codes and best practices. *Corporate Governance, 15*(6), 1030–1037.

Charan, R. (2005). Ending the CEO succession crisis. *Harvard Business Review, 83*(2), 72–81.

Coffee, J. C., Jr. (2002). Understanding Enron: It's about the gatekeepers, stupid (Columbia Law and Economics, Working Paper No. 207). *Business Law, 57,* 1403.

Coffee, J. C., Jr. (2003a). Corporate gatekeepers: Their past, present, and future. (Duke Law School, Working Paper No. 7). *Duke Law Journal, 7.*

Coffee, J. C., Jr. (2003b). What caused Enron? A capsule social and economic history of the 1990s (Columbia University Law School, Working Paper No. 214).

Coggin, P. (2004, October 18). Big investors want SRI research: European institutions to allocate part of brokers' fees to "nontraditional" information. *Financial Times* (UK).

Coombes, P., & Wong, S. C.-Y. (2004). Chairman and CEO—one job or two? *McKinsey Quarterly, 2,* 42–47.

Crystal, G. (1992, January 21). SEC to push for data on pay of executives. *Wall Street Journal,* A-3.

Dashboards in the boardroom. (2006, October). *Directorship, 32*(9), 23–26.

Davis, I. (2006, November 1). Maximizing shareholder value doesn't cut it anymore. *Knowledge@Wharton.*

Dodd, M. E. (1932). For whom are corporate managers trustees. *Harvard Law Review, 45,* 1145–1163.

Drucker, P. F. (1974). *Management: Tasks, responsibilities, and practices* (Abridged and Rev. ed.). Oxford, UK: Butterworth-Heineman.

Easterbrook, F. H., & Fischel, D. R. (1991). *The economic structure of corporate law.* Cambridge, MA: Harvard University Press.

Edwards, F. R. (2003, October 30–November 1). *U.S. corporate governance: What went wrong and can it be fixed?* Paper prepared for the B.I.S. and Federal Reserve Bank of Chicago conference, "Market Discipline: The Evidence across Countries and Industries," Chicago.

Ellsworth, R. R. (2002). *Leading with purpose: The new corporate realities.* Stanford, CA: Stanford University Press.

Environmental Finance. (2007, August 16). Pressure grows on U.S. companies to act on climate. *Environmental Finance Magazine.*

Equilar. (2008). *2008 CD&A overview report.* Red Shores, CA: Author.

European Corporate Governance Institute. (1992). *Report of the committee on the financial aspects of corporate governance.* Brussels, Belgium: Author.

Fama, E. (1988). Agency problems and the theory of the firm. *Journal of Political Economy, 88,* 288, 291–293.

Fama, E. F., & Jensen, M. C. (1983a). Agency problems and residual claims. *Journal of Law and Economics, 26,* 325–344.

Fama, E. F., & Jensen, M. C. (1983b). Separation of ownership and control. *Journal of Law and Economics, 26*(2), 301–325.

Favole, J. A. (2007, January 10). Big firms increasingly declassify boards. *Wall Street Journal,* Eastern Edition.

Felton, R., & Fritz, P. (2005). The view from the boardroom: Value and performance [Special issue]. *McKinsey Quarterly,* 48–61.

Freeman, R. E. (1984). *Strategic management: A stakeholder approach.* Boston: Pitman.

Freeman, R. E., & McVea, J. (2001). A stakeholder approach to strategic management. In M. Hitt, E. Freeman, & J. Harrison (Eds.), *Handbook of strategic management* (pp. 189–207). Oxford: Blackwell.

Friedman, M. (1970, September 13). The social responsibility of business is to increase profits. *New York Times Magazine,* 32–33, 122, 124, 126.

Gillan & Martin. (2002). Financial engineering, corporate governance, and the collapse of Enron. WP 2002-001, Center for Corporate Governance, University of Delaware.

Gillies, J. (1992). *Boardroom renaissance.* Toronto: McGraw-Hill Ryerson and the National Centre for Management Research and Development.

Gordon, J. N. (2003). What Enron means for the management and control of the modern corporation: Some initial reflections. *University of Chicago Law Review, 69*(3), 1233–1251.

Hall & Murphy. (2002). Stock options for undiversified executives. *Journal of Accounting and Economics, 3,* 42.

Hansen, P. (1993, August). The duty of care, the business judgment rules, and the American Law Institute Corporate Governance Project. *Business Lawyer, 48,* 1355–1359.

Hawley, J. P., & Williams, A. T. (2001). *The rise of fiduciary capitalism in the United States.* Philadelphia: University of Pennsylvania Press.

Heidrick & Struggles. (2006). The board of directors' role in CEO succession, Q & A with Heidrick & Struggles. In *Building high-performance boards.* Chicago: Author.

Hinsey, J. (2006) Corporate governance activists are headed in the wrong direction. *Working Knowledge,* Harvard Business School.

Holland, K. (2005, May). Review of the book *Corporate governance: Law, theory and policy. Law and Politics Book Review, 15*(5), 444–448.

Ide, R. W. (2003). Post-Enron corporate governance opportunities—Creating a culture of greater board collaboration and oversight. *Mercer Law Review, 54*(3), 838.

Institute of Internal Auditors. (2006). *The audit committee—purpose, process, professionalism.* Altamonte Springs, FL: Author.

Institutional Shareholder Services. (2006). *Corporate governance: From compliance obligation to business imperative.* Global Institutional Investor Study. Rockville, MD: Author.

Jensen, M. C. (2001). Value maximization, stakeholder theory, and the corporate objective function. *European Financial Management Review, 7*(3), 297–317.

Jensen, M. C., & Meckling, W. H. (1976). Theory of the firm: Managerial behavior, agency costs and ownership structure. *Journal of Financial Economics, 3*, 305–360.

Jones, D. E. (2007). Corporate crisis: The readiness is all. *Heidrick & Struggles Governance Letter.* Chicago: Heidrick & Struggles.

Joo, T. W. (Ed.). (2004). *Corporate governance: Law, theory and policy.* Durham, NC: Carolina Academic Press.

Kaldor, M., Anheier, H., & Glasius, M. (2003). Global civil society in an era of regressive globalisation. In M. Kaldor, H. Anheier, & M. Glasius (Eds.), *Global civil society 2003* (pp. 3–33). Oxford: Oxford University Press.

Keinath, A. K., & Walo, J. C. (2004, November 23). Audit committee responsibilities: Focusing on oversight, open communication, and best practices. *The CPA Journal, 74*(11), 22–29.

Khurana, R., & Cohn, J. (2003, Spring). How to succeed at CEO Succession: Aligning strategy and succession. *Directorship, 29*(5), 7–11.

Khurana, R., & Pick, K. (2005). The social nature of boards. *Brooklyn Law Review, 70*(3), 1259–1285.

Klein, W. A. (1982). The modern business organization: Bargaining under constraints. *Yale Law Review, 91*, 1521.

Kleinman, B., & Thompson, G. L. (2002). *Corporate responsibility: The board of directors' duty of oversight, Parts I and II.* Dallas, TX: Haynes and Boone.

de Kluyver, C. A., & Pearce, J. A., II (2009). *Strategy: A view from the top* (3rd ed.). Upper Saddle River, NJ: Prentice Hall.

Korn/Ferry International. (2007). *33rd annual board of directors study.* Los Angeles: Author.

Leighton, D. S. R., & Thain, D. H. (1997). *Making boards work.* Whitby, Ontario: McGraw-Hill Ryerson.

Lindstrom, D. (2008). Enron scandal. *Microsoft® Encarta® Online Encyclopedia*.

Lipton, M., & Savitt, W. (2007, May). The many myths of Lucian Bebchuk. *Virginia Law Review, 93*(3), 733.

Lorsch, J. (1995, January–February). Empowering the board. *Harvard Business Review, 73*(1), 107–117.

Lorsch, J. (with MacIver, E.). (1989). *Pawns and potentates—The reality of America's corporate boards*. Watertown, MA: Harvard Business School Press.

Lucier, C., Kocourek, P., & Habbel, R. (2006). CEO succession 2005—The crest of the wave. *Strategy and Business* (Booz Allen Hamilton), *43*.

Macavoy, P. W., & Milstein, I. (2003). *The recurrent crisis in corporate governance*. New York: Palgrave Macmillan.

Mace, M. (1971). *Directors: Myth and reality*. Boston: Division of Research, Harvard Business School.

Martin, R. (2003). The coming corporate revolt. *Compass*, The Center for Public Leadership, John F. Kennedy School of Government, Harvard University.

Matheson, J. H., & Olson, B. A. (1992). Corporate law and the long term shareholder model of corporate governance. *Minnesota Law Review, 76*, 1313–1391.

McCarroll, T. (1992, May 4). The shareholders strike back: Executive pay. *Time*, 46–48.

MCI, Inc. (2008). *Microsoft® Encarta® Online Encyclopedia*.

McKinsey & Company. (2006, March). *What directors know about their companies: A McKinsey Survey*.

McTaggart, J., Kontes, P., & Mankins, M. (1994). *The value imperative—Managing for superior shareholder value*. New York: Free Press.

Mercer Delta Consulting. (2006). *Mercer Delta 2006 governance survey*. New York: Author.

Millstein, I. M., Gregory, H. J., & Grapsas, R. C. (2006, January). Six priorities for boards in 2006. *Weil Briefing: Corporate Governance*. New York: Wel, Gotsal & Manges.

Monks, R. A. G. (2005, March). Corporate governance—USA—fall 2004 reform—the wrong way and the right way. *Corporate Governance, 13*(2), 108.

Morgan Lewis Counselors at Law. (2004). *Corporate governance: An overview of recently adopted reforms*. Washington, DC: Author.

Nadler, D. (2004). What's the board's role in strategy development? Engaging the board in corporate strategy. *Strategy and Leadership, 32*(5), 25–33.

Nadler, D., Behan, B., & Nadler, M. B. (2006). *Building better boards: A blueprint for effective governance*. San Francisco: Jossey-Bass.

Nash, J. (2008, March 28). CEO pay: Performance-based bonuses down, discretionary bonuses up in '07. *Financial Week.*

National Association of Corporate Directors (NACD) in collaboration with Mercer Delta Consulting. (2006). *The role of the board in CEO succession.* Washington, DC, and New York: Author.

Petra, S. T. (2006). Corporate governance reforms: Fact or fiction. *Corporate Governance, 6*(2), 107–115.

PricewaterhouseCoopers. (April 2007). *Convergence of IFRS and US GAAP.* New York: Author.

Reason. (2005, October). Print edition.

Redefining the role of the chairman of the board. (2002, December 18). *Knowledge@Wharton.*

Rérolle, J.-F., & Vermeire, T. (2005, April 29). M&A best practices for boards of directors. From Houlihan, Lokey, Howard, & Zukin, *Corporate Board Member Magazine,* M&A/Capital Markets.

Rivero, J. C., & Nadler, D. A. (2003). Building a valuable relationship between CEOs and their boards. *Mercer Management Journal.*

Rochlin, S. (2006). The new laws for business success. *Corporate Citizen.*

Romano, R. (1994). *Politics and pension funds.* New York: The Manhattan Institute.

Rose, N. & Wolfram, C. (2002). Regulating executive pay: Using the tax code to influence chief executive officer compensation. *Journal of Labor Economics, 20*(2), S138–S175.

Salwen, K. G. (1992, February 14). Shareholder groups cheer SEC's moves on disclosure of executive compensation. *Wall Street Journal,* p. A-4.

Saxby, J., & Schacter, M. (2003). *Civil society and public governance. Getting a fix on legitimacy.* Ottawa: Conference Board of Canada.

Spencer Stuart. (2007). *Spencer Stuart board index 2007.* New York: Author.

Spencer Stuart, Board Services Practice. (2008). *Cornerstone of the board—the nonexecutive chairman: Offering new solutions.* New York: Author.

Splitting up the roles of CEO and chairman: Reform or red herring? (2004, June 2). *Knowledge@Wharton.*

Springer, J. D. (1999). Corporate law and constituency statutes: Hollow hopes and false fears. *New York University Annual Survey American Law,* 122.

The state of the corporate board, 2007. (April 2007). A McKinsey global survey, *McKinsey Quarterly.*

Stewart, J. K., & Countryman, A. (2002, February 24). Local audit conflicts add up: Consulting deals, hiring practices in question. *Chicago Tribune,* p. C-1.

Sundaram, A. K., & Inkpen, A. C. (2004, May–June). The corporate objective revisited. *Organization Science, 15*(3), 350–363.

Thornton, E. (2002, January 14). The bids sure are getting hostile: Unsolicited offers are on the rise in a market ripe for consolidation. *Business Week*.

United Nations Conference on Trade and Development (UNCTAD). (2004). *The shift towards services*. World Investment Report 2004. Geneva: Author.

Waller, Lansden, Dortch, & Davis, LLP. (2005, June 24). The board's role in risk management. *Corporate Board Member Magazine*.

Wood, D. (2005). *Red flags in management culture, strategies, and practices.* National Association of Corporate Directors.

Index